RACHMONES

The Passion

of

Hebraic Empathy,

a History

Burt Alpert © 2010

AuthorHouse™

1663 Liberty Drive, Suite 200

Bloomington, IN 47403

www.authorhouse.com

Phone: 1-800-839-8640

© 2010 Burt Alpert. All rights reserved.

No part of this book may be reproduced, stored in a retrieval system, or transmitted by any means without the written permission of the author.

First published by AuthorHouse 574/2010

ISBN: 978-1-4490-9730-1 (sc)
ISBN: 978-1-4490-9732-5 (e)

Library of Congress Control Number: 2010927300

Printed in the United States of America
Bloomington, Indiana

This book is printed on acid-free paper.

Around 5000 years ago, an unusual assortment of defiant souls began drifting into the land then known as Canaan. Defectors from bronze-age empires in surrounding areas that now include Turkey, Iraq, Iran, Syria, Lebanon and Egypt, sheepherders and dirt farmers, they settled on the semi-arid soil of Palestine. Drawn from the variety of ethnic groups in the states from which they had come, they brought with them a heritage of the hunter-gatherers and early farmers whose culture had been forcibly suppressed in the emerging empires. Initially regarding them as a minor pestilence, the states from which they had fled spoke of them as habiru *- "stateless citizens." In time merging their diverse backgrounds into a new ethnicity,* habiru *became hebrew.*

Out of the customs that the habiru *had evolved together, they developed a society of their own, with a code of behavior that preserved a passion for universal empathy - in hebrew,* rachmones. *After several centuries, a man of extraordinary vision formulated the code into law. That law became a marker, continuing down to our own day as a touchstone for humanitarian justice. The empathetic heart of it would inspire three world religions, Judaism, Christianity and Muhammadanism, and in its secular expression, "Liberty, Equality, Fraternity."*

This is their story, that of a people known to their neighbors as the habiru, *and of the visionary in their midst, a man named Moses, who transformed the basis of their existence. As once again I poured through the Bible and the ancient archives that had been preserved from the lands thereabout, truth is, the story pretty much wrote itself. Pressed between the tales of mythic fantasy that priestly scribes had deemed it desirable to contribute, I read in amazement as the People of the Book told their own story, and then saw it corroborated in things that others anciently had written about them. It was a thrilling experience, the essence of which I've tried to convey.*

The story goes on to reveal the fate of this people upon remaking their society in the image of those from which they had fled. It is my story too, for in recovering a likely truth of their lives, I unearthed something of my own.

rach.mo.nes. rach as in Bach - mu.nis

טוֹב שְׁפַל-רוּחַ, אֶת-עֲנִיִּים (עֲנָוִים);   מֵחַלֵּק שָׁלָל, אֶת-גֵּאִים.

"Better it is to be of a humble spirit with the lowly,
than to divide the spoil with the proud."
- Proverbs. 16.19

Contents

I A Grand Awakening

It began with a dream. "*Joseph dreamed a dream, and he told it his brethren . . . For, behold, we were binding sheaves in the field, and, lo, my sheaf arose , and also stood upright; and, behold, your sheaves stood round about and made obeisance to my sheaf. And his brethren said to him, Shalt thou indeed reign over us? . . . And he dreamed yet another dream . . . Behold, I have dreamed a dream more; and, behold, the sun and the moon and the eleven stars made obeisance to me.*"

Exasperated by his lofty presumption, Joseph's brothers sell him to a passing caravan of spice merchants on their way to Egypt. They in turn sell Joseph to Potiphar, captain of the Pharaoh's guard. Recognizing Joseph's special abilities, Potiphar soon appoints him to be head slave in his household. "*And his master saw that the Lord was with him, and that the Lord made all that he did to prosper in his hand . . . And he made him overseer over his house, and all that he had he put into his hand.*"

Falsely accused by Potiphar's wife of sexual assault, Joseph is thrown into the Pharaoh's prison. Here too his skills are quickly recognized. "*And the keeper of the prison committed to Joseph's hand all the prisoners that were in the prison; and whatsoever they did there, he was the doer of it.*" Appointed chief trustee, Joseph's services will soon be even more handsomely rewarded.

Brought from the prison to interpret Pharaoh's dreams, Joseph predicts: "*Behold, there come seven years of great plenty throughout all the land of Egypt. And there shall arise after them seven years of famine.*" What is to be done? "*Let Pharaoh do this,* and let him appoint officers over the land, and take up the fifth part of the land of Egypt in the seven plenteous years. . . And that food shall be for store to the land against the seven years of famine in the land of Egypt."

Pleased with Joseph's plan and impressed by his ability, Pharaoh appoints him to the highest office in the land. "Thou shalt be over my house, and according unto thy word shall all my people be ruled. Only in the throne will I be greater than thou. And Pharaoh said unto Joseph, See, I have set thee over all the land of Egypt. And Pharaoh took off his ring from his hand, and put it upon Joseph's hand, and arrayed him in vestures of fine linen, and put a gold chain about his neck. And he made him to ride in the second chariot which he had; and they cried before him, Bow the knee, and he made him ruler over all the land of Egypt."

As anticipated, the famine arrives. "And when all the land of Egypt was famished, the people cried to Pharaoh for bread, and Pharaoh said unto all the Egyptians, Go unto Joseph; what he saith to you, do. . . And Joseph opened all the storehouses, and sold unto the Egyptians; and the famine waxed sore in the land of Egypt. And all countries came into Egypt to Joseph for to buy corn," Joseph's brothers among them, "because that the famine was so sore in all the lands."

As the famine progresses, year by year, Pharaoh's capital accumulates. "And Joseph gathered up all the money that was found in the land of Egypt, and in the land of Canaan, for the corn which they bought, and Joseph brought the money into Pharaoh's house.
"And when money failed in the land of Egypt, and in the land of Canaan, all the Egyptians came up to Joseph, and said, Give us bread . . . And Joseph said, Give your cattle, and I will give you for your cattle, if money fail. And they brought their cattle unto Joseph, and Joseph gave them bread in exchange for horses, and for the flocks, and for the cattle of the herds, and for the asses, and he fed them

with bread for that year.

"When that year was ended, they came unto him the second year, and said unto him . . . Our money is spent. My lord also hath our herds of cattle. There is not ought left in the sight of my lord, but our bodies, and our lands. . . Buy us and our land for bread, and we and our land will be servants unto Pharaoh. . . And Joseph bought all the land of Egypt for Pharaoh, for the Egyptians sold every man his field . . . So the land became Pharaoh's.

"And as for the people, he removed them to cities from one end of the borders of Egypt even to the other end thereof . . . Then Joseph said unto the people, Behold, I have bought you this day and your land for Pharaoh; lo, here is seed for you, and ye shall sow the land. And it shall come to pass in the increase, that ye shall give the fifth part unto Pharaoh . . .

"And they said, Thou hast saved our lives. Let us find grace in the sight of my lord, and we will be Pharaoh's servants." [1]

One can say many things about this story, speculating in a variety of ways as to its meaning. The circumstances under which it might have been set down can be examined at length. For what reason was it recounted, to what end, and with what relation if any to historical events? Whatever the truth of the tale or its source might be, the import is clear. A rather arrogant but uniquely talented young man, sold as a slave, succeeds in having himself appointed chief in the house of his master, then made first trustee among his jail mates, and finally invested as second in command after the king himself. In effect, by dint of extraordinary service in all three positions, the young man rises from the rank of slave to that of prime minister. In this capacity he succeeds in acquiring all the cattle and private holdings in the land for the king, in making the former landholders royal servants, and relocating them in administratively designated settlements.

Looking past the sacred context in which the story is told to examine its bald reality, one can observe Joseph transforming an entire populace of free farmers into bounden employees of the royal state. On behalf of the Pharaoh, Joseph has, in a word, instituted a system of state capitalism. A remarkable accomplishment, not often thought of in this way, it is most readily understood in terms of the corporate realities of the age. Rachmones was not part of those realities.

.

Rachmones, I remember as having been the single word that probably carried the greatest import in my early life. While comparable in its sense to pity, sympathy, empathy, compassion, mercy, tenderness, fellow-feeling and caring, Hebraic rachmones embraces a wider perspective than any of these. One of my favorite song lines assures the listener that, *"When something's wrong with my baby, something's wrong with me."* [2] More broadly than this, though in the same vein, with rachmones anything that happens anywhere to anyone happens to oneself. In rachmones, the heart is infinitely open to hurts wherever they occur. I often heard my sainted grandmother use the word, and when she did it came from some place deep within an abdomen that had been well worn with the delivery of many offspring, the sound of it mounting through her throat as the word passed out into a call for limitless mercy.

"Let not mercy and truth forsake thee," the reader is admonished in *Proverbs* 3.3. *"Bind them about thy neck, write them upon the table of thine heart."* One carries rachmones about as a talisman for one's soul.

In its openness to a world of feeling, rachmones can be a source of infinite possible enrichment. A gentle breeze upon one's cheek, a kiss thrown from afar, the touch of a child's hand, so much resonates in the vaults of a warm heart. All things are possible in fully exercised rachmones, all joys are accessible.

Benefitting by this freedom of emotional sensitivity, rachmones also then weighs down upon one's shoulders as a burden that, however one may will it, can never be discarded. All living creatures are born into suffering, the Buddha asserted as a first principle, therefore to all one must have compassion. Rachmones needs no such reminder. For in rachmones the suffering of any living creature is one's own suffering. It is something felt from inside rather than reasoned out.

No wonder that the descendants of the ancient Hebrews have as their national monument a Wailing Wall. One goes there to cry for all the sorrows that have been brought down everywhere upon everyone. However unthinking and often selfishly that I may have led my life, and however little at most times I may have been aware of it, the spirit of rachmones has never ceased to be an inseparable element of my being.

In what kind of culture, and under what circumstances, could a trait such as this have emerged? And how are we to reconcile so great a sense of caring, as is suggested in rachmones, with Joseph's celebrated instrumentality in the separation of a people from their land and their delivery over to the state?

Whatever the answer, one may also take note that this is the same culture which produced a most remarkable trio in our own times, arguably three of the four seminal thinkers of the modern era. In physical science, Albert Einstein; in behavioral science, Sigmund Freud; and in political economy, Karl Marx. The son of an apostate Jew, Karl nevertheless, if ungraciously, revealed his roots in his first published work, "On the Jewish Question." Labor, sex and relativity fairly well spans the parameters of the human experience. Remarkably, a culture that includes roughly .3% of the population, that's 3/1000ths, presented the species with three of the four figures whose writings most influenced contemporary thought and understanding. The fourth of course was Charles Darwin, quietly an atheist. In addition then to the apparently stark contrast between the workings of rachmones and the ministerial agenda of the biblical Joseph, in fathoming the inner reality of Jewish culture, we need also to consider its unique intellectual contribution.

There is the other side of course. Choosing the "Jewish question" as a title for his thesis, Marx lit upon a phrase that's haunted the west ever since one of its prophets was nailed to a cross. For two thousand years the Jews have been a perpetual thorn in the side of western society. At the deepest levels of the social contract, they refused to join up, nor, however one pummeled and defamed them, would they go 'way. The "poisoner of all peoples," Adolph Hitler called "international Jewry" in the closing sentence of his "last testament" on April 29, 1945, the day before he committed suicide. An extreme statement from a crazed mind, it nevertheless echoed sentiments that have been familiar enough throughout the western world.

The "Jewish story is a source of endless irritation," Abba Eban observes introducing his study of the Jewish heritage. "It refuses to fit the doctrinal mold and thus incurs a great deal of academic hostility. Jewishness is a notion that extends across the graveyards in which other civilizations are buried." From an ordinary western perspective, the Jews have ever seemed to be an altogether strange and irreconcilable people. This and their persistent recalcitrance in the face of repeated persecution, count among additional traits that have kept the "jewish question" very much alive. They are also to be considered in comprehending the driving force within Jewish culture.

What were the origins, then, we might ask in Darwinian terms, out of which the "Jewish question" evolved? What the cauldron, and what the fire in which this culture was forged, that from it so disparate an array of aptitudes and contributions might have come forth? What is the common thread in Jewish culture, if we may put it simply, that connects two such strikingly variant personalities as Joseph and

Einstein, one a liberator of minds, the other an architect of servitude?.

Concluding his work, Eban asks, "Why do so few people have so large a voice, so that whatever men do and think and say to this very day has been profoundly affected by the Jewish experience?" [3] The nature of the answer, I think, can be gleaned from the magnitude of the question. *For, if Jewish culture has indeed had so profound and widespread an impact, then almost certainly it must have emerged from a background that was much greater than itself, and which it has served, in turn, as a repository of values and practices that were more widely observed than merely among the Jews.*

Searching for the answer, then, I found myself compelled to return to a time when neither Jews nor their Hebraic antecedents existed. In an alchemical allusion that is more than coincidental, the cauldron boiled that the children might come forth.

.

It's only in the past several years that I've become aware of the impact of rachmones in my personal life and in the life of the Jews. Fortunately for me having been her favorite grandchild, I was very deeply affected by the workings of rachmones through my experiences with my grandmother. Indeed, though one might be hard put to locate the spirit of rachmones in any obvious way in the everyday relations of the family members by whom I was surrounded as I grew up, looking back on things now I can see it operative everywhere under the surface.

True, aunts and uncles squabbled furiously, even bitterly, with each other and intergenerationally as well. At the age of 14, in 1940, I remember seeing Lillian Hellman's play, *The Little Foxes* on Broadway, and thinking, Why, with their spitefulness and bickering, they're no different than my family. It was something of a surprise to learn that ours was neither more nor less dysfunctional than other families in America. Still in all, we were bound by a sense of mutual acceptance and caring that made us unquestioningly comfortable in each other's presence. We may have been subject to as much emotional parsimony as any other American family of the '30s and '40s, but not to the emotional reserve that seemed to characterize so many.

While I can't recall my mother telling me that she loved me, she was never ever cold towards me, or for that matter, towards anyone else. She never shut me out emotionally, or traded affection for obedience. Without thinking about it, I had an inherent sense of being permanently held in her heart and mind. Anyone who has seen the face of a parent tightly drawn into an image of cold severity in response to an exhibit of behavior that displeased them, can appreciate the significance of enjoying freedom from coldness in one's upbringing. The steely frigidity of *American Gothic* had no place in the Jewish life to which I was accustomed. Submerged as it may have been beneath dispute and acrimony, in our family as in those of my friends, a preserve of rachmones was perpetuated.

That heritage, I realize now, was very much at the roots of an inquiry upon which I embarked early in my life. Along with many other youths of my age, I believed that people were inherently good. Feeling it in myself, I wanted to believe it in everyone. I now have another way of looking at the proposition of species goodness. It's come at the end of a long search. At the time, however, my determination to discover evidence of peaceable collaboration among human beings sent me wandering for years through ancient texts and modern commentaries.

One misty day in San Francisco I turned a corner in my quest. There by chance in the fog-bound reading room of the State College library, I came upon *Paleolithic Art*, Paolo Grazioso's 1956 survey of the hunter-gatherer paintings that adorned dark cave walls in southern France and northern Spain. Here, in these elegant paintings, that Picasso didn't hesitate to acclaim as a universe of masterpieces, I viewed for the first time something immensely different than anything I'd ever seen before. Page after page glowed with images of mammoth and bison standing stalwartly in an immensity of presence, horses racing along certainly and swiftly, and great red deer lightly lifting into the air.

At once both unpretentiously substantive and eerily luminous, something in the way these ancient animals had been depicted suggested a state of peace and mindfulness in the artists who had created them. A spirit of goodness shone through the paintings that intimated the existence of a quality of life for which I had been looking. Through the affection, respect and acceptance with which the animals were portrayed, a sense of rachmones was reflected, I would now say, a spirit of community with other creatures, that resonated with the deepest feelings of my upbringing. During subsequent years, the acquaintance that I acquired with Western archaeology would fully confirm the joyful epiphany with which I was blessed that day in the college library. It was in the unearthing of ancient things that I would one day discover an answer to the "Jewish question."

.

For perhaps twenty thousand years, down to about 10,000 b.c. a vast, unified culture ranged across Europe and Asia. From the foothills of the Urals to the farthest western shores of Portugal, a distance greater than the breadth of the North American continent, a common culture prevailed. Neither bound by conquest nor plagued with tribal warfare, its peoples for the most part shared a quality tool kit and artistic expression. The sublime beauty of the great beasts painted on cave walls in the west was reflected eastward in the steppes with the erection of large, communal, mammoth bone dwellings. Pelvic and leg bones, skulls and vertebrae were stacked and interlaced in architectonic perfection to provide a framework for skins that sheltered the dwellers within. Like the exquisitely shaped spearheads that members of this culture flaked, the mammoth-bone homes were as much works of art as they were products of technical excellence. Without benefit of aristocracies, bureaucracies or warrior armies, the cultural life of these Cro-Magnon hunters and gatherers streamed seamlessly through time and space. [4]

Their livelihood centering around the chase of the great red deer, woolly mammoth and bison, the species had emerged from among all the others with a sense of itself in the midst of the rest. In them, we may with good reason assume, homo sapiens' cognizance of its own unique standing in the world of creatures and plants first fully came alive. There were mammoth, bison, horses, reindeer, lions and bears, and there was a culture of master hunters that stretched along with them, side by side, over a course of more than 3000 miles. Having evolved during countless thousands of years of survival and transformation, it was a grand awakening of the human spirit. Here in a burst of startling awareness, Western society, from Portugal to Pakistan, had its start.

Following in the tracks of so extraordinary an achievement, mesolithic times traditionally have suffered from a bad press. Gone were the splendid paintings, gone the exquisitely crafted bone and ivory carving. In its place, when I went to school, we were offered images of ragtaggle bands drifting aimlessly from place to place, scrounging nuts in the forest and cracking shells along the sea shore, leaving behind in their wake a chaotic litter of kitchen middens. It was a short and miserable existence.

In fact, it's now understood, this transitional era between paleolithic hunting and neolithic farming must have been a most exciting time in the passage of human consciousness. With the retreat of the glaciers and a warming of the weather, the old hunting culture traded their wooden spears for the far more efficient and effective bows and arrows. Canoes, skis and sleds were added to their inventory as needed. Miniaturizing their tool kit, they settled in the variety of ecological niches that sprang up with the passing of the cold. In response to local habitats, the trans-european culture of the big game hunters diversified, laying down the ancestral roots of peoples and nations that were soon to follow. [5]

The change in thinking from species awareness to locally rooted consciousness must have been momentous. Human figures proliferate in rock art. With a heightened sense of self and other, deliberate burials become frequent. Here and there intentional cultivation is initiated. Nowhere, however, the evidence now suggests, were the new arts of planting and harvesting so fruitfully pursued as around the fertile shores of a great, inland lake that one day would become the Black Sea.

During the last glacial period the straits of the Bosporus that lie between the Black Sea and Mediterranean Sea had been closed. The salt waters of the Mediterranean could make no contact with the immense sweet water lake, the future Black Sea, that lay beyond. From east to west, four great rivers flowed into the lake - Don, Dnieper, Dnestr and Danube, along with numerous lesser ones. The lake served as a temperate wonderland for the hunter-gatherer migrants who settled about it. The waters teemed with fish, the hills roundabout provided ample game, fruits and grains were readily available for cultivation. The lake was an eden. In fact, as is becoming increasingly clear, it was almost certainly the site of the Garden of Eden that would linger in the memories of the many peoples who emerged from around its shores.

About 7000 b.c., deep into the heart of central Turkey, settlers from the southern shores of the lake had founded Çatal Hüyük, the earliest known town in the world. On the western shore of the lake, part way up the Danube at the Iron Gates, from around 6000 b.c., stood the remarkable village of Lepenski Vir. Thought to have served as a kind of retreat, its residents, fishing salmon from the narrow gorge of the Iron Gates, often reached the age of 70.

Ancient Greeks would commemorate the eastern shore of the lake in some of their earliest legends. The range of the Caucasus provided the lake with its eastern border. To a lofty peak in these mountains Zeus would chain Prometheus - "Forethinker/First Craftsman," the Firebringer, for presuming to have saved a portion of humanity from the "great flood" that Zeus had visited upon them, as well for having played on the greed of the Lord of All in cheating him out of his share of the spoils. It was here too, across the "unfriendly waters" of the Black Sea, that Jason and the Argonauts, initiating Greek mercantile piracy, would come to carry off Medea, so talented in herbal witchery, along with the Golden Fleece - proposed by some to have been the hardy winter wheat of the Kuban.

Through the mountain passes of the Caucasus the ancient Hurrians, and possibly also the earliest gypsy tinkerers and fortune tellers, would descend to bring Turkey, Mesopotamia and the Near East much of its metallurgical expertise and mythic legend. To this day the Black Sea slopes of the Caucasus are home to the longliving Abkhasians with their exceptional culture, stretching from the shores of the great salt sea up the slopes of the Caucasus mountains, growing and harvesting at all levels for the most varied diet in the world.

Upland from the southeast corner of the lake, at the juncture of Turkey, Iran and Armenia, towering into the sky at 17,000 feet, stood Mt. Ararat. It could well have served as a major landmark for the early hunters/farmers fleeing the rising waters of the vast lake around which they made their home. For around 5500 b.c., with glacial melt raising water levels everywhere, the Gates of the Bosporus were breached. The Mediterranean poured through, and the Great Flood of ancient western legend was on, sending migrants scurrying in all directions. [6]

Within 200 years farm settlements appeared all along the Mediterranean coast from Greece to Spain. In Europe, in Asia, wherever they went, the survivors established communities that would soon enough evolve into ethnic centers. In all these places, archaeological finds reveal, the peaceable craftsmanship of the big game hunters was preserved in the stream of human consciousness that these first farmers brought with them. [7]

Not for long, however, for a fundamental break in the culture of the western world would soon come down upon the heads of the intrepid homo sapiens. The ancient ties of community that passed in time from hunter-gatherers to the first farmers would face an assault they could not withstand. Firmly based upon monopolies in the forging of bronze tools and weapons, the age of empire was on its way. With it an unusual league of dissenters would appear.

II Benefits and Obedience

We tend to think of the Bronze-Age empires in purely political terms. Indeed, this is the way that histories, both academic and popular portray them. Potentates vie for imperial control, array armies against each other, poison their predecessors, launch campaigns of conquest, suppress rebellions and so on. All this of course happened, and continued to be the ordinary state of affairs right on down to modern times. Beneath the unending dramas of intrigue and betrayal, however, that ricocheted through the halls of royal courts lay a stubborn reality upon which all the action turned.

The imperial houses functioned in fact as corporations in which the king or emperor served as head of state, chief executive officer and major shareholder. The evidence is out front and abundant.

In the city-state of Mari, reign of Zimrilim, time of Hammurabi, Palace rations are issued for woodworkers, leather workers, reedworkers, scribes, singers, husbandmen, gardeners, cooks, attendants, shepherds, wagon drivers, millers, wood carvers and *"young ladies."* The king's holdings included *"tin of the palace,"* *"cows of the palace,"* *"fields of the palace,"* *"plows of the palace,"* etc. "The monarch was at the same time a great proprietor." [8]

By the 29th year of his reign, from the lands he has captured and seized, Hammurabi himself has awarded fiefdoms to lapidaries, scribes, soothsayers, singers, goldsmiths, masons, woodworkers, metalsmiths, weavers, basket makers, bird catchers, shepherds, fishermen, palace guards, temple personnel, soldiers and supply chiefs to provide for their needs in exchange for service to the palace. His portfolio diversified to the max, the king had things sewed up every which way, horizontally and vertically.

The king of pre-Phoenician Ugarit in Lebanon collected taxes on grain, oil, beverages, oxen, sheep, asses, grazing, transit and occupations. He received *"offering money"* and *"gifts"* along with obligatory service on crown lands, fortresses and temples. "The main source of his income . . . was derived from the crown lands which the king amassed by expropriation as a result of victorious wars, by confiscation and by purchase." [9]

At Alalakh in Syria, King Ammitaku loans silver to "individuals on the security of the debtor, himself, his wife, his sons, who *'as surety must dwell in the house of Ammitaku,'*" to work off the debt. If they escape or die the debt is transferred to another relative. The king buys up debts owed by one citizen to another under the same arrangements, buys entire villages, collects interest of 20-25%. [10]

At Pylos in Mycenaean Crete about 1200 b.c. palace records tabulate the distribution of a ton of bronze to be worked by some 400 smiths in two dozen towns and hamlets. [11] "It is the most obvious lesson of archaeology, now confirmed by the Linear B Tablets, that the Mycenaean Greeks were great men of business." [12]

Among the Hittites, "An important part of the booty were the skilled craftsmen who lived in conquered towns. They were deported to Hittite territory and settled there to serve the needs of the conqueror in palace or temple." [13] In Assyria, "Captive craftsmen were deemed so valuable an asset that they were placed on the list of booty second only to princes and state officials." [14]

In *Genesis* 34.10, Jacob is described as being involved in trade and real estate, Abraham with cattle trading, gold and silver. King Solomon, "The wise ruler of Israel was a copper king, a shipping magnate, a merchant prince, and a great builder." [15] The House of David in Judah functioned as a corporate entity, so did the House of Omri in Israel and various other "houses" throughout the Near and Middle East, down to our own times, as in the House of Rothschild.

I could go on. It's apparent in effect that the Fords and Rockefellers, Mitsubishis and I.G. Farbens of their times, these early imperial magnates ran things with as much economic finesse and political panache as the oil barons of *Dallas* and the wine dynasts of *Falcon's Crest*. If anything, what with ramified money-lending schemes, hired help supplemented by slave labor, land-grabbing and expropriation, and so on, imperial corporations were even more effective in wrapping up the economy than are those today.

In our own democratic societies, economic dynasts rely on the crazy-glue of campaign contributions and lobbyists in cementing politicians to their enterprises. Bronze-Age potentates were faced with no such problems. Thanks to arrangements such as those reputedly devised in Egypt by Joseph for the pharaoh, the exercise of economic and political domination was united in a single person, the ruling potentate. He, and on one or two occasions she, was the state, and so the prevailing forms of capital accumulation amounted to varieties of state capitalism. [16]

As may be judged in the Code of Hammurabi, the enforcement of corporate control over the populace was rigorous. The consequences visited upon the supporters of rival dynasts was implacable. While princes and skilled workers might be taken into captivity, defeated soldiers and people alike were treated to arson, impalement, decapitation and whatever form of homicide and degradation was deemed to be most impressive in convincing would-be rivals of the hopelessness of their cause. Graven in stone, the proudly displayed accounts of victorious dynasts attest as much. *"Many soldiers I have captured alive,"* the Assyrian Ashurnasirpal II boasts around 875 b.c., *"of some I chopped off the hands and feet; of others the nose and ears I cut off; of many soldiers I destroyed the eyes; one pile of bodies while yet alive, and one of heads I reared up on the heights within their town . . . Their boys and their maidens I dishonored, the city I overthrew, razed and burned with fire."* [17]

With the military-industrial complex combined in a single personage within the walls of the royal palace, war itself was already big business. In the taking of Lachish in southern Palestine, 701 B.C., the Assyrian dynast Sennacherib employed helmeted warriors wearing bronze-plated vests, advancing behind wooden barricades and brazen shields, in armored vehicles and elevated siege machines. Engraved for all to see upon a wall of the magnificent palace that Sennacherib built at Nineveh, the scene depicts an early chemical warfare division pouring hot oil down upon the heads of the enemy. Defenders are shown being impaled naked in the streets. [18]

From whatever aspect one examines it, whether political, economic or social, Bronze-Age society clearly marked a significant, not to say traumatic, departure from the predominantly egalitarian, collaborative and peaceful culture of its hunter-gatherer and early farming antecedents. Corporate realism signaled the passage of the species into another state of being in the evolution of its psyche. The transition was profound, and for better or for worse, things would never be the same.

Blood flowed. Hearts were torn from chests, foreskins were sliced from the uncircumcised dead, ears and hands chopped away and brought home in sacks and baskets, the unborn cut from their mothers' wombs. With the perfection of the corporate state during the reign of Augustus, malcontents, dissenters and rivals were crucified in long lines on both sides of the Appian Way, "queen of roads" that led to Rome, there to rot in the sun and be torn apart by vultures. The lesson was highly visible, and not at all subtle. Any limits to the vengeance that dynasts imposed upon defeated opponents were defined solely by the political-economic interests of the dynasts themselves.

Nevertheless, no more than it is now, the struggle to impose corporate society upon tribal and village economies was not readily settled. *"Not all the households of the poor are equally submissive,"* a Sumerian scribal student observed, probably quoting a common saying on his practice tablet. Those who did submit might on the other hand find themselves the object of popular scorn. *"The dog wags his tongue at a millstone,"* another saying went, *"and says to his companion: 'I will put an elegant leash on it.'"* [19] The dog takes pride in his servitude, pretending it to be a lovely thing of his own devising. Less graciously than the scribe who copied this gem of self-delusion, a modern desperado might well have retorted, "I don't need no stinkin' badges."

The spirit of collaborative existence, sown so deeply in the lives of hunter-gatherers and early farmers, lingered in hearts everywhere. In Sumeria the earliest of all marriage contracts stipulates that *he will be to her as a husband and a brother, and she will be to him as a wife and a sister.* A thousand years later a Song of Solomon would bear witness to the tradition in declaring, *"How fair is my love, my sister, my spouse."* The species had come alive in a collaborative spirit. During a million years or more of trial and error in survival, the value of communal harmony was built into the human psyche. Denying the existence of the collaborative impulse is an insult to one's integrity. It registers as an injury both to body and to spirit. [20]

In addition therefore to merciless acts of repression that alternated with employments and distributions from the royal larder, rulers had good reason to promote the righteousness of their corporate control. The shattering of collaborative society needed to be justified. Belief was vital if people were to accept the new order into which they had been rudely inducted. Over the harsh certainties of the stick and the blandishments of the carrot, in Arnold Toynbee's inspired metaphor, the sweet and plangent notes of the lyre soon were sounded. In a carefully constructed mythic ideology an offering of hope was extended.

In ancient Mesopotamia, then, whether in Assur, Ur, Uruk, Nineveh, Babylon or elsewhere, the ideological takeover of popular consciousness was implemented in a grand drama that has come down to us in a text which scholars have chosen to tag the *Epic of Creation*. Once a year, at the time of the *Akitu*, New Year's festival, it was incumbent upon anyone desiring to assert corporate kingship over the community in Mesopotamia to stand before the people and gird himself in the fighting adornments of the warrior god Marduk. Playing the principle role in an annual ceremony of mythic ascension that was enacted year after year, it would be his task to slay the monstrous Tiamat and her dragon son, Kingu.

"The story's final goal," Thorkild Jacobsen remarks, "is certainly Marduk's attaining to the position of permanent king of the universe, thereby creating the monarchical form of government." This quite clearly was the intent of the *Enuma elish* - "When on high," as from its opening words, the epic struggle was known to the Sumerians. Its dramatic presentation was indeed aimed at substantiating monarchy, and it was something more. For in promoting its ideology of kingship, the drama aimed at the same time to purge the minds of the populace for once and for all of any favorable thought they might have regarding the collaborative society from which they had come. "A major step toward making this possible," Jacobsen goes on to say, was Marduk's "vanquishing Tiamat in a decisive victory for energy and movement." [21] Each year, this is the way the year would begin.

Tiamat and Kingu, "energy" and "movement," female and male principles of life and community. From the seed of her husband, *Apsu* - the primeval Abyss, Tiamat, also known as "Chaos," gives birth to the *"all."* Out of this formless storehouse of begetting and becoming from which all comes and to which all returns, the *Enuma Elish* goes on to tell us, Tiamat generates *"bogs and islands,"* the places of life on earth, as well as the heavens and even the gods themselves. Recollecting the reverence in which the female principle was held by hunter-gatherer and early farming peoples, Tiamat is recognized as having been Mother of All. She was the genetrix. And more.

Tiamat's name appears cognatively in Hebrew as *yam* - the salt "sea." Mother of all, Tiamat is more specifically then the Mother of Waters. Naming her thus, the *Enuma Elish* is preserving ancient evolutionary wisdom that appears in a variety of forms among many early cultures. "Familiar to people all along the coast of West Africa," she is celebrated in the Vodun/Voodoo cult of Mami-Wata, as she is known in Afro-pidgin. [22] Among natives of central Mexico she is Mistress of Waters. Sitting by the sides of lakes and streams everywhere over which they are guardians, nymphs are Tiamat's daughters.

If Marduk is to establish order in the land, Tiamat must go. First drugging Apsu into complacency and then killing him, Marduk next slays Tiamat. Continuing his impersonation of the warrior-god, the king *"let fly an arrow, it split her belly, cut through her inward parts and gashed the heart. He held her fast, extinguished her life."* Pierced and gutted, the great Tiamat, mother of waters and genetrix of all, is dead. Her immensity is laid waste.

In the passing of the Mother of Waters and her radiant spouse, the cultural energy of the hunter-gatherers and early farmers will be put to rest. So too will her "Chaos." Chaos of course is the pejorative word in which organically derived organization is familiarly belittled and defamed. Western society had persisted peacefully for 25,000 years or more without the benefit of imposed regulation. Regarding this purely collaborative state of affairs with abhorrence, the corporate ethos intends installing an alternative point of view. From a corporate perspective, things are held to be chaotic until proper order prevails. Marduk will bring that order about.

Where however will the victorious monarch turn in creating his new order? The only source of energy available is the freshly slain carcass of Tiamat. Dead or alive, she is the source of the All. And so, *"The lord stood upon Tiamat's hinder parts, and with his merciless club he smashed her skull . . . He split her up like a flat fish into two halves."* Out of the hinder half of the sundered Mother of Waters, Marduk creates a *"covering for heaven,"* installing within it the starry constellations. From her upper half he fashions the things of earth. Heaping a mountain over Tiamat's head, Marduk pierces her eyes to form the sources of the Tigris and Euphrates. To make the waters flow, he then *"drills fountains"* through her *"dugs"* - she is after all animalian, beastly and monstrous. The pornography of violence starts here, it appears, coeval with the earliest policies of domination. Torn apart in an act of matricide, the fertile energies of hunter-gatherers and early farmers are dedicated to installing the heaven and earth of the corporate order. Needless to say, it will be a quite different heaven and earth than Tiamat's had been.

Magicians still "saw the lady in half." That is their job, while ours is to watch in submission and fright. How reassuring, then, when she emerges unscathed from the assault upon her, still whole, intact. We sigh with relief, and the lady, scantily clad, demurely curtsies, desirable as ever. Property of the magician. [23]

A complementary fate awaits Tiamat's dragon son Kingu. The monster of all monsters is bound and handed over to the God of Death. Marduk then *"took from him the Tablets of Destinies, not rightfully his, sealed* [them] *with a seal and fastened* [them] *on his* [own] *breast."* As much as Tiamat stood for the "energy" of the populace, Kingu represented their "movement." Honored in Asia rather than slain as in the west, Kingu is the self-empowered dragon of all possibilities. Having in corporate eyes no claim on righteousness, he has been rendered powerless. It is the corporate ruler now, no longer the populace, who will determine destinies.

Nor is this an end to Kingu's usefulness. Marduk calls an assembly of the gods, and indicts Kingu as an instigator. The gods oblige. *"They bound him [Kingu] . . . inflicted the [death] penalty on him, severed his arteries, and from his blood he [Marduk] formed mankind, imposed toil on man, set the gods free."* The gods in this scenario are easily recognizable in the persons of those who will manage the new order. In support of that order, mankind is to be a hewer of logs and a carrier of water. The flesh of the mother has been fashioned to create the things of heaven and earth, conformably to corporate order. Its animal vitality crushed, the blood of the dragon will run through corporate arteries. Once generated by consensus within the community, decisions will be handed down by executive order. It's the system.

No longer masters of their own destinies, the energy and movement of the populace are both now exclusively in the hands of the dynast. People's skills, the pride they took in creations of their own making, their ability to work together, even in many instances the affection that once they exercised within their communities of hunter-gatherers and early farmers, traits that had embellished their life, all now will be dedicated to the service of the corporate monarch. The connective tissue of collaborative society has been torn apart, its spirit quenched, its flesh and blood reallocated to the maintenance of corporate production and royal administration. On more than one cylinder seal the god of the ruler, or the ruler himself, will be depicted riding the back of the dragon over the subdued waters of the dragon's mother. [24]

Triumphantly gleeful, the gods decree a new mandate for Marduk. *"Benefits and Obedience"* will be posted as spears on either side of his throne. In the twin dictates of this decree, for four millennia, down to and including our own times, the corporate matrix will manage the social order according to its own needs. NOVUS ORDO SECULARUM - a "New Order for the World," the reverse of the U.S. dollar bill announces. Celebrating the ascension of the most awesome corporate structure in history, now spread out across the face of the entire globe, the declaration on the dollar bill is placed beneath a Masonic emblem of pyramid and shining eye. The order that Marduk initiates in the mythic slaying of Tiamat is the order that Joseph establishes for Pharaoh. Under an eye and a pyramid it watches still over corporate culture.

Something else needs to be taken care of. One final scene remains to be staged in order that the festival of the New Year may be complete. In then comes *Ishtar* - "bright star," all bells and bangles, clothed in whirling gossamer pants, a saltire framing her ample breasts. Later to be known as Venus, she's star both of dawn and of dusk, first to arrive and last to leave, sparkling from evening till morn with hope for the needy. The high priestess, or perhaps the *"first lady of the harem,"* the queen herself, plays the part of Ishtar, the *"Queen of Heaven, pure torch that flares in the sky, heavenly light, shining bright like day . . .* [who can] *set the poor folk going at their dances."* Setting the folk dancing, however, will not be her purpose this day.

"Bridegroom," Ishtar says, addressing the victorious warrior-god Marduk in the person of the king, *"lion, dear to my heart, goodly is your beauty, honeysweet. You have captivated me, let me stand tremblingly before you, bridegroom. I would be taken by you to the bed-chamber."* [25] The newly invested chief of corporate operations needs no persuasion. This is the moment above all for which he has been waiting, and he will seize it.

"Grant him a pleasant reign to come!" Ishtar's handmaidens enjoin her. *"May he like a good shepherd make the folds teem, may there be vines under him, may there be barley under him, may carp flood the river beneath him . . . may deer multiply in the forests . . . watered gardens bear honey and wine . . . lettuce and cress grow in the vegetable plots . . . O my lady, queen of heaven and earth . . . may he live long in your embrace."* [26]

Reconstituted as Ishtar, the slain Mother of all fecundity has returned, now bestowing her favors of green fields and abundant game upon the chief of the corporate palace. He, not a freely engaged populace, will be the beneficiary of their efforts. Goddess, virgin or saint, people may still pray to her in the many forms that she will assume. The distribution of "benefits," however, will remain firmly in the hands of the corporate ruler, living long in her embrace.

Kingu too will be remembered. Not just for two thousand years in the annual Akitu festival, but for all times. Wherever the bestial dragon of collaborative impulse appears, he will be slain. By Perseus in Greek legend, by Beowulf and Siegfried, by St. Michael and St. George in Christian scripture, followed by a whole host of intrepid knights-errant. Meanwhile, by way of Pan, his creative attributes are transferred to a cloven-hooved, serpent-tailed, horned figure, the true believers' Devil.

And so it is done. The contention between chaos and command has culminated in a clear victory for corporate order. The animal spirits of the Mother of Waters and her son the terrible Dragon have been vanquished and anathematized. Driven from the state and out of the body, a pair of exorcised demons, they have been declared outcasts from acceptable awareness. In the wake of their passing, they leave an orderly and obedient society. In a lapse of inner conviction, the legendary mantle of the *Enuma elish* passes on to the Jews. As the main characters in a little morality tale of benefits and obedience, Marduk will become Mordecai, Ishtar will be Esther.

Corporate monarchs readily grasped the need to safeguard their mandate of obedience by something more substantial than the mythic justification that was provided in the Akitu festival. One after another, therefore, they devised codes of law. Benefits were guaranteed in rules and regulations that established wage rates, principles of ownership, procedures for restitution and the like. In return, obedience would be encouraged through varieties of punishment. The celebrated Code of Hammurabi stipulated instances in which an eye would be plucked out, an ear sliced away, a hand cut off, repeated beatings inflicted and, most often, the taking of one's life for infractions of the established order. An Assyrian code of laws attributed to Tiglath-Pileser I, but probably earlier, ordered cutting off both nose and ears, slicing off the lower lip across the blade of an axe, mutilation of the entire face, flogging with staves, pouring pitch over the head, tearing out both eyes and of course death penalties. Buttressing the mythologically seductive tones of the lyre, the effectiveness of the carrot and stick, nicely summarized in "benefits and obedience," had been institutionalized.

.

The combined potency of carrot, stick and lyre notwithstanding, disaffection was widespread. Not everyone appreciated the corporate order that had supplanted their prior existence. Memories abounded of a Golden Age and a Garden of Eden in which milk and honey freely flowed as once they had around the shores of the Black Sea lake. Messiahs would appear everywhere, offering to lead people in a return to the peace and harmony they had once enjoyed, a promised land that lay forever over the rainbow.

Prayers for deliverance to gods and goddesses went up on all sides. *"O star of lamentation,"* a plea to Ishtar began, *". . . O Lady of heaven and earth, shepherdess of the weary people . . . I have cried to thee, suffering, wearied, and distressed . . . See me, O my Lady; accept my prayers . . . Pity! For my sickened heart which is full of tears and suffering . . . How long, O my Lady, shall my adversaries . . . rage against me? . . . My family is scattered, my roof is broken up . . . Accept my prayer, loosen my fetters, secure my deliverance . . . How long, O my Lady . . . ?"* [27]

Forsaking reliance on the power of prayer, more than a few of the distressed and weary took matters into their own hands. While monarchs sent armies scurrying every which way, battling each other and lesser stakeholders in their efforts to diversify and expand their corporate sway, people were fleeing to the hills, out into the steppes, and farther on. Others left the land of their birth to serve as contract laborers or mercenaries elsewhere. Many packed up their goods and their animals and roamed the countryside, free of taxes and corvée labor on the irrigation ditches. Brigandage sprang up everywhere.

The *Laws of Eshnunna*, from Tell Asmar, the site of a city-state around 1800 b.c. offhandedly decree what will befall him, *"If a man hates his town and his lord and becomes a fugitive."* An execration text from Egypt, around 1790 b.c. calls down curses upon the heads of *"All* [Egyptian] *men, all people, all folk, all males, all eunuchs, all women and all officials . . . who may rebel, who may plot, who may fight, and who may talk of fighting, or who may talk of rebelling, and every rebel who talks of rebelling in this entire land."* The chronicle of Nergalushezib, after mentioning that the populace of Elam has risen up and slain the king there, notes dismally that, around 700 b.c., *"For eight years there was no king in Babylon."*

A tablet of Assyrian prophecies predicts that *"the ruler will be slain during an uprising . . . Revolution, chaos and calamity will occur in the country. A dreadful* [man], *son of a nobody will arise . . . Cities will decay, houses* [will be desolate]. *Revolution, destruction will occur."* It's safe to assume that these dire prophecies in the breakdown of corporate order were based upon memories of actual events. In a prayer that he had delivered around 1310 b.c. to the Hattian [Hittite] Storm-god along with the rest of the gods, the Hittite king Mursilis attests to the reality of such breakdowns: *"O gods, take ye pity on the Hatti land! On the one hand it is afflicted with a plague, on the other hand, the Arzawa land, each one has rebelled . . . Moreover, those countries which belong to the Hatti land, the*

Kashean country . . . Arawanna . . . Kalasma . . . Lukka . . . Pitasea: these lands have also renounced the Sun-goddess of Arinna. They cast off their tributes and began to attack the Hatti land in their turn." [28]

At times and in places, even within the heavily policed heartlands of the state, disillusionment with the benefits that obedience yielded erupted in outright rebellion. Some of it was recorded in ancient texts. Complaining that *"we are hungry,"* in 1171 b.c. workers on the royal tombs in Egypt staged a series of strikes. In 413 b.c. the 20,000 state slaves who worked the silver mines of Attica for Athens rose up and fled the country. In the third of the Servile Wars, a revolt of 200,000 slaves in Sicily held Roman armies at bay from 144-133 b.c. Freeing slaves with an emancipation proclamation as they fought up and down the Italian peninsula, the homespun army of the gladiator Spartacus defeated Roman legions one after another, until vanquished in 71 b.c. Pompey celebrated the victory. [29]

Beyond the confines of the cities and guarded lands whose orderly daily life is so artfully portrayed in illustrated history books, for two thousand years the entire region was in turmoil. Amidst these turbulent events the Children of Israel staged their Exodus from Egypt. The way had been paved for them. Centuries earlier, around 1725 b.c.., contemporary with the reign of Hammurabi, a cuneiform tablet with an anxious dispatch reaches Zimri-Lim, king of the city-state of Mari. *"All the Benjaminites raised fire signals . . . All the cities of the Benjaminites of the Terqa district raised fire signals in response."* So far, the message nervously continues, *"I have not ascertained the meaning of these signals."* Are the Benjaminites preparing to flee? Will they attack? The writer intends to find out. In the meantime, he suggests, *"Let the guard of the city of Mari be strengthened, and let my lord not go outside the gate."* [30]

Here, in this tersely worded warning of imminent danger sent to a local corporate monarch, we hear of the earliest and in fact the only historically attested mention of a group of people that the Hebrews would later claim as having been among the twelve tribes of their progenitors. They are outsiders, they are a threat and they are capable of the sort of brigandage that assailed corporate strongholds everywhere in the region. Though the dispatch to Zimri-Lim does not say as much, they are easily counted among the *habiru,* a widely spread people of their day who were causing trouble wherever they appeared. As though in confirmation of their identity, another dispatch informs Zimri-Lim that two thousand *"Hapiru of the land"* have been recruited as security forces to guard a settlement on the banks of the Euphrates for a rival to the king. There are more signal fires. During the succeeding centuries the habiru/hapiru, converging from everywhere in the Bronze-Age empires, will develop a culture that the Children of Israel will find awaiting them when at last they enter the Holy Land.

Drenched in blood and brutally suppressed, rebellions came and went, without appreciably altering the operations of corporate order. Rebellion of course indicated that people wished something else in their lives other than authoritarian control. In their hearts there still dwelt a spirit of social harmony and self-expression that they carried within them since the species came truly alive in the days of the hunter- gatherers. That spirit was a human heritage, and, resisting the fiercest repression, it persisted everywhere in people's lives. Rebellion, however, lacked an effective expression of consciousness and an alternative social infrastructure which, when taken together, could effectively guarantee the perpetuation of a disaffected culture.

Nonetheless, in one particular place, the Western life-stream of a sociable society would be articulated in awareness and preserved in an ethos of behavior. Within the corporate existence that bounded it on all sides, a spirit of rachmones fell heir to the illuminated existence of the hunter-gatherers and early farmers. In a single paramount injunction, *"Thou shalt love thy neighbor as thyself,"* [31] these cultural descendants of the first westerners intended nothing less than totally to replace the social order of benefits and obedience.

III Born in Dissent

At least as mentioned in texts of the time, the people responsible for the idea and practice of rachmones had a rather unpromising beginning. We first hear of them in Syria about 2200 b.c. They are habiru/hapiru. In Egypt their name takes the form of 'pr and 'pr.w, the hyphen indicating a hard H and the w a plural, transliterated as 'Apiru. Appearing almost simultaneously in Mesopotamia, Egypt and among the Hittites and Hurrians in Turkey, the original language of their name is shrouded in mystery. It might have arisen anywhere from the slopes of the Zagros to the banks of the Nile, as these people themselves did. In Sumerian logographic form they are frequently referred to as SA-GAZ, a term likely derived from the Akkadian *saggasu* - "attacker/aggressor" or "killer/murderer," probably in turn related to Akkadian *habbatu* - "migrant/vagrant." Pillaging the established settlements of Bronze-Age empires, SA.GAZ soon became an epithet, whatever the context, for "murderers," of whom there were great numbers, most prominently the habiru themselves, throughout the region.

It is hard to overlook a connection between Hebrews and habiru. In the canonical *Pentateuch,* the Five Books of Moses, the Hebrews are spoken of as *ibrim/ivrim.* Since one finds Eber, a son of Shem, in the *Pentateuch,* Eber rather than habiru is sometimes cited as a lineal source of the Hebrews. This genealogy, however, could easily have been inserted at a much later date by parties concerned with cleaning up the origins of their ancestors. Whatever the intent of the authorities who wove ancient folk tales into sacred text, when "Hebrews" are mentioned, rather than children of God, Israelites, etc., they appear as foreigners. When Abraham arrives in Canaan as a foreigner after the infamous occasion when he traded his *"sister"* Sarah into the harem of the Pharaoh in exchange for *"sheep, and oxen, and he asses, and menservants, and maidservants, and she asses, and camels,"* he is identified as *"Abram the Hebrew."* [32]

With an internationally common root phoneme of *pr/br,* the circumstances of their entry into history makes the identity of *hapiru/habiru, 'pr.w, ibrim/ivrim, Hebrews* all but certain. In many texts, habiru is customarily used in the sense of "refugees/foreigners /emigres," with no prejudicial implications. Among the Hittites the verb for "flee" is *ih-bi-ar,* related to habiru. Foreigners in the lands where they are mentioned, and citizens of none, it has been suggested that far from being an ethnic designation, their name meant literally "stateless citizens," a political term that was employed throughout the Near and Middle East for the better part of two millennia to describe a social group that heralded the likelihood of disturbance wherever they appeared.

The ethnically diverse background of the habiru is reflected in the tirades of the furiously inspired Ezekiel. When God, through the agency of the prophet, wishes to admonish the corrupt and arrogant Jerusalemites of the poverty of their origins, he reminds them, *"Thy birth and thy nativity is of the land of Canaan. Thy father was an Amorite, and thy mother was an Hurrian."* [33] The Amurru/Amorites were Western Semites. The Hurrians were Caucasoid. In the land of Canaan a mix of the impoverished rebellious gathered together and jelled to produce a new ethnicity.

In the psalm with which he dedicates the Ark of the Covenant, David recalls the days of the Israelites, *"When ye were but few, even a few, and strangers in it* [Canaan]. *And when they went from nation to nation, and from one kingdom to another people."* [34] One could hardly ask for a more apt description of an assemblage of international runaways and stateless citizens.

The ethnic mix continues into later times. Fleeing from Egypt after slaying an Egyptian guard, Moses marries Zipporah, a

Midianite woman. Occupying land east of the Jordan, the Midianites were Arabic sheep herders and traders. David himself was the great grandson of Boaz and Ruth, a Moabite woman. Also across the Jordan, and speaking a language closely akin to Hebrew, Moabite customs were nevertheless distinctly foreign to those of the "children of Israel." Ruth's legendary allegiance to the Israelite Naomi earns her a book of her own in the Hebraic canon. For his part, David as king, in a fit of infatuation marries Beth-sheba after exposing her husband Uriah the Hittite to death in battle. The Hittites were Indo-European. David and Beth-sheba's son, Solomon, would take wives from many lands.

In sum, habiru appear in the texts as "people having loosened or sundered the ties that bound them to their country to follow a more vagrant life, and who habitually hired out their services . . . above all as soldiers, but who were perhaps also able to exercise on their own behalf their talents in brigandage and raids, whence the early defamatory name of SA.GAZ which remained attached to them in Sumerographic writing." [35] Vagrants, mercenaries and brigands, that they were, as the ancient texts will show, the habiru were also something much more. ***Most of all, they were dissenters. They began their existence as runaways, they came from all the lands in the early western Bronze-Age world where corporate rule was being imposed, and they held in their hearts an outlook on life that was being extinguished everywhere around them.***

■

Of the many things I've been called in my life, most seem to cluster around one central attribute. *Akshen* and *shunya* were the earliest, my mother's choice in Yiddish, when I was six years old to describe my "contrariness." An *akshen* is a "stubborn ox," refusing to be moved or go along with what was desired. *Shunya* signified my mischievousness. Other soubriquets followed over the years. Gadfly, shitkicker, rebel, maverick, outlaw, free spirit, all suggest an attitude of dissent.

Born into an era of intense personal analysis, for most of my life I looked to family circumstances in accounting for my dissident nature. Rebellion against Pavlovian upbringing by my mother, jealousy of my younger sister, and so on. An *akshen* and *shunya* in her own way, my mother was famous for returning purchases that on second thought didn't quite match her tastes. The butt in an excess of bureaucratic adjustment, she once found herself overwhelmed with three bicycles from Macy's. At least within the family, my contrariness was perhaps predictable.

Then too, there was my Uncle Joe. My father having died when I was five, Joe adopted me as a sometime surrogate parent, settling into my budding awareness in the role of a male model. With world revolution in the air, Joe joined the Communist Party. A painter of portraits and landscapes, he soon became embroiled in a bitter argument with party head, Earl Browder. The party line at the time was to drape scenes of American life with as many dark and muddy hues as possible, thus demonstrating the poverty of existence in this stronghold of capitalism. With an unfailing sense of color, Joe balked at the mandate, dubbing it, with a sneer that I can remember to this day, the Ashcan School. Quitting the party, he became a dissenter to the second degree.

My personal heritage, as I understood it in those days of burgeoning psychologistics, had easily then prepared me for my own wanderlust into dissidence. Embarking upon a lifetime of ideological rebellion, I found satisfaction in shattering the sacred cows of commonly accepted beliefs, poking holes in the professionally accredited theses of academic authorities, contending for righteousness with bureaucratic administrators, corrupt politicians and overworked store clerks. Along the way I resigned a fleet appointment to Annapolis, and turned my back on a prestigious future at Columbia University. Contemporary psychology might now classify me as having suffered from "oppositional defiant disorder," with a "penchant to defy authority."

For decades, I never felt myself a part of the mainstream culture that flowed cheerfully enough past me. I pitied Babbitt with his Main Street mental set, scorned celluloid heroes such as Cary Grant and James Stewart, despised Dick Tracy and Little Orphan Annie, had no stand-up cheers for great plays on the baseball diamond and no applause for passing parades of baton--twirling, pom-pom girls in mini skirts. I didn't really think of myself as an "American."

A dissenter from American culture, I had little use either for Jewish ceremonies, prayers or ritual. Growing up in a working-class Jewish neighborhood in the east-central Bronx, my close friends were all Jewish. None of us, however, was a practicing Jew, nor were our families. Looking back on those years now, I can see that we were Jewish enough to disaffect from the outward trappings of religion. They seemed to us more a denial of our birthright than an affirmation. I knew I was Jewish. We all did. Jewishness however never occurred to us as something to think much about. My own sense of being Jewish did not penetrate very far beyond an awareness of the doors that were closed to me. Perhaps as a measure of self-defense as much as from ideological conviction, I didn't feel all that put out over the exclusion. I had no desire to be either a greater or lesser Gatsby, hob-nobbing with the likes of Tom and Daisy. While I envied the life to which they had access, I had no wish to be part of it, "careless people" who "smashed up things and creatures." What lay on the other side of the doors did not particularly attract me.

Dissenting from so much, I belonged to so little. A vale of distance, much of it still remaining, separated me from the world around. Not surprisingly, most all the moments when I found community centered about acts of rebellion. A sit-down strike in Brooklyn, 1954, when 200 of us took over the American Safety Razor Plant, cafeteria included, in a vain attempt at preventing the company from running-away to Virginia. A voluntary union organized during the Summer of Love in the San Francisco Dept. of Social Services. Disdaining political alliances and declining invitations to join the

AFL-CIO, we campaigned as effectively for the right to self-expression within the welfare system as the flower children manifested outside in the streets and parks of the Haight-Ashbury. Seven annual Rainbow Gatherings, where thousands of us made camp in a wilderness area and celebrated July 4th as a liberation from the compliance and conformity that national holiday represented to others.

Now in my later years, I'm very much part of a warmly vibrant community on the Big Island of Hawaii. At the same time, I've come to appreciate the consonance between the personal and social sources of my life, its dissention and its longings. Still in search of roots, and pursuing my maverick inclinations into their biblical background, I came upon Moses in the act of smashing the tablets of the Ten Commandments. The Mosaic demonstration of holy defiance became a benchmark of heritage that took me far deeper into an understanding of my origins than family life had. Never mind that they were written in the fiery hand of God Himself, the tablets had to go. The idol of the Golden Calf would be smashed, ground up and pulverized. In that momentous event, memorialized in popular consciousness as strikingly as the parting of the Red Sea, I caught my first glimpse of the social deeps from which my personal endowment of dissent had emerged.

I'd heard too of the habiru. Confronting the realities of habiru rebellion, the full import of my heritage finally came home to me, offering me a place in the world in which I can take pride. Shot through as they were with contradiction and connivance, opportunism and infamy, the actions of the habiru were nevertheless inspired by a determination to reject the blandishments of "benefits and obedience" that were being adopted as a way of life all around them. Sifting through those of the ancient texts that have survived for clues to their struggles and achievement, laid open the wellsprings of rachmones and dissent in which I've made my own being. It's a relief to realize that my wayward and often overreactive "contrariness" can be traced back to the contentions of a people who refused to be taken in by the newly minted institutes of authority.

Throwing light as it did on the roots of my personal dissent, a survey of habiru rebellion also quite naturally offered insights into the origins of Hebraic culture and sources of the "Jewish question." Examined in detail, the trials, tribulations and triumphs of the habiru, the dynamics of their involvement with the corporate empires from which they fled, clarifies a great deal about Jewish life. It also adds much, I believe, to understanding the qualities of humanity that we so cherish in our species. Returning to the ancient texts and biblical accounts with which I'd become cursorily acquainted many years earlier, I found a great deal that amplified my previous impressions in ways that I little expected. Still, I was totally unprepared to discover half a millennium of habiru struggle culminating finally in an inspired vision of extraordinary magnitude.

.

"These unclothed people who travel in dead silence." Thus the passage begins describing the habits of the SA.GAZ/habiru in a dispatch that was sent around 2020 b.c. to Shulgi, king of Ur during the Sumerian Third Dynasty. *"As for their men and their women,"* the dispatch continues, *"their men go where they please, their women carry spindle and spinning bowl. Their encampments are wherever they pitch them. The decrees of Shulgi, my king, they do not obey."*

Wearing whatever scraps of clothing are available, or that they themselves devised, carrying with them only the basic necessities, in "dead silence" they defy authority by evading it. Making camp where it suits them, they enjoy a quality of freedom that was hard to come by in the domains of "benefits and obedience."

On other occasions the SA.GAZ may choose to apply for employment. Sumerian documents show them receiving rations of cattle and sheep from royal livestock. They may even accept positions of military authority. In the first year of Rim-Sin, king of Larsa, about 1820 b.c., we hear that: *"Four suits of clothing for the sergeants of the Hibiri* [were] *received by Ibni-Adad . . . out of the* [temple] *treasury of Bit-Shamash."* As so often happened in early corporate history, temples of the gods served as banks for the holdings of ruling dynasts. "In God we trust," the U.S. dollar bill assures us.

When necessity arose, contract labor could be obtained in the estates of the wealthy. In the outlying province of Hurrian Nuzi, northern Iraq, around 1450 b.c. We learn that, *"Warad-kubi is an Assyrian habiru, of his own free will, in capacity of a servant, into the house of Tehiptilla . . . he has entered."* Taribatum, an Akkadian habiru also signs into the employ of Tehiptilla. A habiru woman, Wahuluki likewise engages herself and her children in service to the same Tehiptilla. *"Wahuluki of Seqarum, herself, of her own free will, with her children, in the capacity of servant and servants, to Tehiptilla she has delivered."* Should Wahuluki break the contract, both she and her children will be subject to punishment as drastic as anything laid down in the Code of Hammurabi. *"If Wahuluki breaks the agreement and from the house of Tehiptilla goes out, saying, 'I, I am no longer a servant and my children are no longer servants,' then Tehiptilla from Wahuluki and her offspring will tear out the eyes, and will sell them."* With draconian penalties evidently imposed at all levels of corporate society, entering into labor agreements must have been in many cases a last resort. Better to head for the hills, or the open steppe.

A letter from Enna-Assur, perhaps a merchant of Hittite Alishar in north-east central Turkey, about 1890 b.c., hints at a climate of common concern among the habiru. *"In regard to the gentlemen, habiru of the palace, belonging to Salashuwa, who are in prison,"* Enna-Assur writes to his colleague Nabil-Enlil. *"If they do not wish to return them, ransom these gentlemen. Whatever ransom for them that the palace demands from you, in* [your] *message let me know, and I will send it to you . . .* [These] *gentlemen have abundant* [silver] *for ransom."* Details of the imprisonment of these habiru are lacking. Probably contract laborers of Salashuwa who he placed in service to the palace, they evidently have acquired resources of their own. Enna-Assur is confident they will repay him the "ransom" money when set free.

As happens sometimes with rebels, the habiru occasionally attracted well-off, disaffected sympathizers. A prince of Alalakh in northern Syria deserts and spends 7 years with the SA.GAZ. Serving them as interpreter of bird flights and reading signs from the intestines and livers of lambs, he contributes his knowledge of the royal art of mantic magic upon which corporate dynasts generally relied in planning their military engagements. It seems hardly likely that advice of this sort would have been of much assistance to marauding habiru in conducting the guerilla type of action to which they were accustomed. As we will see, Egyptian governors were amply familiar with the hit-and-run politics with which habiru brigands made their lives miserable. The prince, it appears, was well received.

Very much on the minds of ruling dynasts throughout the region, SA.GAZ/habiru make a regular appearance in Assyro-Babylonian omen texts, characteristically in predictions of disaster. *"Disorder,"* one such text warns, *"the SA.GAZ will be on the rampage."* A Hittite omen text similarly cautions, *"If a halo . . . habiru will enter."* When the heavens are consulted, the Sumerian star *"of the SA.GAZ"* is identified in Akkadian as being *"of the habbatu"* - brigands, and was designated as the star of Nergal. Nergal was Mars in the Sumero-Babylonian celestial pantheon, according the habiru a high compliment by potentates whose entire fortunes depended upon war.

On the other hand, SA.GAZ/habiru are sometimes referred to with esteem, even thought to possess divine powers. At the temple of Adad, an Assyrian list of gods that are to be honored includes *"Habiru"* along with *"Statue of the King."* There is in fact one mention of the habiru as being *"elohim"* - gods themselves.

The habiru evidently impacted the corporate culture of the Bronze Age that spread out from around the Tigris-Euphrates in a wide variety of ways. They sign on for service in armed forces where they may be assigned positions of responsibility, and as contract labor in private households. In return, defectors from established administrations might choose to cast in with them. Upon occasion they are credited with divine powers, and even regarded as divinities in their own right. Unconventionally dressed and incommunicative, they went where they pleased. Above all, they were considered outlaws, a threat to established order, as by their very nature they must have been. The very thought of them induced shudders of impending doom.

So far as Egyptian dynasts were concerned, the habiru were very definitely harbingers of doom. During the latter years of the reign of Amenhotep III through that of his son, Amenhotep IV, nearly 300 troubled letters have survived to report on the exploits of the 'Apiru. Recovered from the ruins at Tell el Amarna, site of the sacred city of Akhetaton that Amenhotep IV established as his seat of power in changing his name to Akhenaton/Ikhnaton, the letters emanate from Syrian, Lebanese and Canaanite kings, princes and governors. One and all, they request assistance against the 'Apiru if the pharaoh wishes Egyptian rule to be maintained.

From Syria we hear Biryawaza complain that an erstwhile Egyptian ally *"gave his horses and his chariot to the 'Apiru."* The disaffection quickly spreads. *"Biridwasa saw this deed and moved Yanuamma to rebellion against me. He took the chariots from Astartu but gave both of them to the 'Apiru."* Desertion soon turns into active rebellion and Biryawaza must flee for his life. *"When the king of Busruna and the king of Halunnu saw this they waged war with Biridaswa against me, constantly saying, 'Come, let's kill*

Biryawaza, and we must not let him go. But I got away from them and stayed in Dimasqa," modern Damascus. Encouraged by defections to the habiru, a pair of local kinglets strip the Egyptian representative of his authority, allowing him just barely to escape with his life.

The news is scarcely better from Byblos, a port on the Lebanese coast. Rib-Adidi, then governor and prince of Gubla/Byblos warns Amenhotep, *"Since the return of your father from Sidon - from his days lands have been going over to the SA.GAZ."* Rib-Adidi names as his arch foe Abdi-Ashirta, a prince of the Amurru/Amorites and a SA.GAZ.

A half century later, the situation has deteriorated to the point where Byblos itself is under siege. *"Look, he strives to seize Gubla!"* Rib-Adidi's successor Rib-Hadda writes excitedly to Akhenaton. *"May the king, my lord, give heed to the words of his servant, and may he hasten with all speed chariots and troops that they may guard the city of the king, my lord . . . But if the king, my lord, does not give heed to the words of his servant, then Gubla will be joined to him, and all the lands of the king as far as Egypt will be joined to the 'Apiru."* While the identity of the chief insurrectionist is not given, he is evidently habiru.

Here for the first time we learn that the habiru of the lands from Lebanon through Canaan and possibly as far as Egypt are acting in concert. The nature of their understanding with each other can only be guessed at. We know that they employed signal fires in communicating information about prospective moves. Whether or not these signals were relayed we are not told. Nor ever do we hear mention of a "high command" among the habiru, or of chosen representatives. While they were joined from time to time by local princes and kinglets, none of them professed to speak for the habiru as a whole. No political infrastructure is ever indicated, though at least towards the time of the Exodus, the habiru in Canaan and perhaps neighboring areas were gathered into clans and tribal affiliations. Twelve Tribes, in the biblical account, though probably more, and extended families within them.

Villages were established in the hill country, possibly many, and there in "high places" communal meals were shared. When Saul comes looking for a seer, presumably to help him locate the asses of his father that had strayed, a young woman at the water well informs him, *"behold, he is here before you. Make haste now, for he came today to the city, for there is a sacrifice of the people today in the high place. As soon as ye be come into the city, ye shall straightway find him, before he go up to the high place to eat, for the people will not eat until he come, because he doth bless the sacrifice, and afterwards they eat what be bidden."* [36]

Sharing a meal in sanctified premises may well have been the earliest habiru custom on the way towards institutionalizing a collaborative society. Undoubtedly an ordinary practice since hunter-gatherer days, this may be its earliest historical notice. Here in this "high place," it is likely that Samuel anointed Saul first king of the Israelites. Subsequent kings both of Judah and Israel would be unrelenting in their efforts to suppress communal gatherings in high places as being contrary to their interests.

For the most part, the picture that emerges from the letters unearthed at el Amarna is one of opportunistic forays carried out by local groups over a wide space, involving dozens of settlements and cities at one time or another. The resistance to corporate rule, continuing as it did over a period of perhaps five centuries implies a coherence of outlook and some sort of cultural understanding. This had very much been the state of affairs among the paleolithic hunter-gatherers. Whereas, however, the cultural unity of the hunter-gatherers arose in a climate of ecologically shared livelihood, the main driving force motivating habiru connectedness was dissent. Coming from different lands and ethnic backgrounds, the habiru had this in common, that they chose not to participate in corporate society.

Writing in cuneiform, a letter from Zimridda of Sidon reveals an even more serious state of affairs than that reported from its northern neighbor, Byblos. *"All the cities that the king gave in my charge,"* Zimridda writes to the pharaoh, *"have gone over to the SA.GAZ."*

More than merely being troublesome in itself, the outlawry of the 'Apiru is fanning rebellion among the trusted satellites of Egyptian imperialism. Inspired by habiru actions, local princes and kings are falling away from the yoke. *"The king of Hasura* [Hazor] *has abandoned himself with the 'Apiru,"* a dispatch despairingly announces from Canaan. *"He has taken over the land of the king for the 'Apiru."* The 'Apiru emerge as firebrands in a conflagration that threatens to spread throughout the region. Wherever taxes, tribute and enforced service is being imposed for the greater enrichment of Nilotic dynasts, habiru resistance is evoking support. Nowhere however is 'Apiru impairment of royal Egyptian domination more widespread than in the land of Canaan, Palestine as we know it today.

"The 'Apiru forces waged war against me," a desperate correspondent writes to the pharaoh, *"and captured the cities of the king, my lord, my god, my Sun."* The habiru appear neither to have been awed by Akhenaton's claims to personal solar divinity nor intimidated by the might of his military forces. *"The 'Apiru captured Mahzibtu,"* the letter continues, *"a city of the king, my lord, and plundered it, and sent it up in flames."*

Pursuing a flexibility of tactics that varied in accord with circumstances, SA.GAZ/habiru serve at times in Egyptian employ, others join rebel leaders, or draw runaway slaves, peasants and state officials into their own ranks. Various writers to the pharaoh accuse each other of being in league with the 'Apiru.

"Let the king know that my youngest brother is estranged from me," Yapahu, prince of Gezer tells the pharaoh. *"And has given his two hands to the chief of the 'Apiru."* Not far from Jerusalem, Shuwardata has a similar tale to tell. *"Let the king, my lord, learn,"* Shuwardata writes, *"that the chief of the 'Apiru has risen against the lands which the god of the king, my lord, gave me. Also let the king know that all my brethren have abandoned me, and it is I and Abdu-Heba [who] fight against the 'Apiru."*

Abdu-Heba, himself prince of Jerusalem, issues a terse warning. *"If there are no archers, the land of the king will pass over to the 'Apiru people."* In a second communication Abdu-Heba's tone betrays mounting concern, mingled with a peevish complaint. *"I will say to the commissioner of the king, 'Why do ye favor the 'Apiru and oppose the governors?'"* Have the Habiru maneuvered Akhenaton into supporting them against his own representatives, or is this a ploy on the part of Abdu-Heba to shame the pharaoh into providing additional assistance? We do not know. At any rate, *"All the governors are lost . . . Send out troops of archers [for] the king has no lands [left]! The 'Apiru plunder all the lands of the king . . . If there are no archers [here] the lands of the king, my lord, will be lost!"*

Abdu-Hebda's pleas become increasingly shrill. *"I have become like an 'Apiru,"* he later writes. *"For there is war against me. I have become like a ship in the midst of the sea . . . Now the 'Apiru capture the cities of the king . . . [The governors] all have perished! . . . Behold Simreda, the townsmen of Lachish have smitten him, slaves who had become 'Apiru."* Lost cities, murdered governors, revolting slaves. Tossed about in all this turbulence, Abdu-Heba feels at sea and adrift, no better than a rootless habiru himself. In one final seizure of despondency, he asks, *"Shall we do like Lab'ayu, who gave the land of Shechem to the 'Apiru?"* He is considering defection.

A rebel prince who has been appointed governor of Shechem, Lab'ayu has evidently been playing a duplicitous game. Biridiya, prince of Megiddo informs the pharaoh, *"Now behold, the two sons of Lab'ayu have given their money to the SA.GAZ and to men of the land of Kashshi to make war against me."* Lab'ayu protests vociferously. In his own communication to Akhenaton, he claims ignorance of the entire affair. *"Pharaoh has also indicted my heir as an 'Apiru,"* Lab'ayu writes. *"I had no idea that my son was consorting with rebels. I have since handed him over to Addaya."*

We've likely lost little in being unable to sort out the truth of these contending claims. Nevertheless the letters that find their way to the imperial capital at Akhetaton make it abundantly clear that, save when supported by a massive show of arms, the infrastructure of Egyptian rule in the Near East was in shambles. However powerful and generally effective its chariots and archers, the corporate culture of Nilotic domination had met its match in habiru dissention.

It would be a mistake to idealize the activities of the habiru. We are no longer in the days of the peaceable paleolithic. A stele erected for Seti I at Beth-shan about 1300 b.c. during his campaign in Canaan contains the information that, *"This day, then, one came to tell his majesty that the 'Apiru of Mt. Yarmut together with the Tayaru . . . are engaged in attacking the Asiatic nomads of Ruhma."* It's hard to image any objective other than plunder in an assault on a band of nomads. Murder and pillage in even the best of causes take their toll on the psyches of the perpetrators, and the habiru were apparently no exception. Making quick and easy kills would have been all the more tempting in the absence of a coherency in outlook and purpose. Packaged into priestly injunctions, surfacing in the Five Books of Moses, facets of the values by which they lived would later be made manifest. For the time being, so far as we know, these adept and persistent habiru brigands who pitilessly harassed Egyptian rule, had yet to articulate those values into a distinctive culture. Westward from the Red Sea, in the heartland of the enemy, that culture would emerge and acquire a voice in a most unexpected fashion.

For hundreds of years, Egyptian armies returned from triumphs in Canaan with habiru prisoners in tow. *"Now the sojourning of the children of Israel, who dwelt in Egypt, was four hundred and thirty years,"* Exodus, 12.40 tells us. So far as the written record is concerned, mention of *pr.w/'*Apiru being in Egypt first appears around 1470 b.c. in contexts which "leave no doubt that in the Nile Valley the pr.w were essentially prisoners of war reduced to servitude." [37] In year 9 of Amenhotep II, 3,600 'Apiru are among some 60,000 captives brought back to Egypt. Sporting an identity that could not quite be classified in ordinary terms, 'Apiru appear in the list of prisoners mid-way between aristocracy and commoners.

Once in Egypt, the 'Apiru were put to work at a variety of tasks. On a stone wall carving in the tomb of Puyemere, a scene intended as comfort for the deceased is titled, *"straining out wine by the 'Apiru."* Ramses III distributes 'Apiru prisoners for service in various temples. At another time a group of 'Apiru are *"given to the god of the temple."* Papyrus Leiden 348 contains instructions to *"Distribute grain rations to the soldiers and to the 'Apiru who transport stones to the great pylon of Ramses II, Beloved-Of-Truth."* 800 'Apiru are included among men who Ramses IV sends to work the quarry in Wadi Hammamat.

Placed into service as plantation laborers, quarrymen, stone carriers, and temple servants, the prospects for captive habiru were not all that bright. Little wonder that their presence encouraged fits of nervousness among their captors. *"Bring in the horses,"* we hear in a message delivered during the reign of Thutmose III, *"or an 'Apiru may pass by,"* and make off with them.

By the time of the Exodus there could well have been tens of thousands of habiru captive slaves and laborers toiling in Egypt. Brought into bondage over a period of 430 years according to biblical chronology, one can imagine their frustration and anger. Having fought for the right to "go where they please," they now drag stones and stomp grapes in the most assiduously regimented of all Bronze-Age societies. Free-ranging brigands, freedom fighters if you will, with names indicating origins anywhere in the Near East - Apir-Baal, Apir-El, Apir-Isis-Satisfied among others, their backs are now bent in service to a social order from which all had fled. Those backs, once covered by brothers in dissent, now are closely watched by the archery police, soldiers who are prepared to shoot down the wayward. Grab a horse or a camel and gallop off into the desert? Probably some do. For the rest, escape is a dream, hardly a reality.

IV A Visionary Transition

"Once you were free men. Neither slaves in the palaces of kings nor servants in the homes of the rich, you came and went as you pleased." Thus he began, haltingly at first, in words that poured from his heart, not entirely knowing where the words would take him. A gaunt figure, he faced the crowd that had come to hear him, guided only by a great vision that burned deeply inside him.

"I am not eloquent," he had confessed, when hearing the voice of the Lord in his vision, and learning of the mission that he was to undertake. *"I am slow of speech and of a slow tongue."* Then the Lord had answered, *"Now therefore go, and I will be thy mouth, and teach thee what thou shalt say."* [38] So powerful was the vision as to overcome even a faltering tongue. Now standing in the midst of the assembled throng he had only to speak, he knew, and the words would come. More than his alone, this was to be the night of the habiru.

.

It seems most likely that Moses' reputed mother Jochebed had contracted for labor in the palace of the pharaoh, and there the child was born. Knowing the infant to be *"one of the Hebrew's children,"* the pharaoh's daughter nevertheless took a liking to him. Deciding to adopt the child, she named him Moses. Nursing him however was out of the question. That would be the task of his natural mother. *"And the maid went and called the child's mother. And Pharaoh's daughter said unto her, Take this child away, and nurse it for me, and I will give thee thy wages. And the woman took the child, and nursed it. And the child grew, and she brought him unto Pharaoh's daughter, and he became her son."* [39]

Adopted into the royal household and benefiting by his station, Moses grew to manhood steeped in royal Egyptian custom and ritual. Still in all, he had been raised by a habiru mother, and so, not surprisingly, he could never feel genuinely at home in his royal surroundings. Dressed in royal garments and engaged in palace pastimes, he was ever something else beneath, harboring a heritage of thought and being that would one day nearly cost him his life. Striving to screen his inner feelings from his outer demeanor, "slow of speech and of a slow tongue," Moses developed a stutter, a defect that was particularly pronounced in the company of Egyptian priests. The royal family laughingly passed off his discomfort, not without reason taking it be a habiru failing, the mark of a bondman in the halls of the mighty. In future reputed dealings with the pharaoh and priests, Moses would appoint his elder brother Aaron, who *"can speak well,"* as his spokesman. A product of radically conflicting cultural backgrounds, this adopted son of royalty would succeed in encompassing both to evolve something that neither alone had possessed. To this end, a long road of personal transformation lay ahead.

Lately Moses had taken to leaving the palace grounds and wandering among other habiru, those perhaps hauling stone or tending the fields. As it is written, *"And it came to pass in those days, when Moses was grown, that he went out unto his brethren, and looked on their burdens."* A not altogether comfortable experience, as captive laborers do not kindly regard one of their own decked out in royal garb. Nevertheless, something was drawing Moses to their company. On one such occasion, *"he spied an Egyptian smiting an Hebrew, one of his brethren. And he looked this way and that, and when he saw no man, he slew the Egyptian and hid him in the sand."* Taken together, the compassion and the murder signaled a major moment of departure from the old life that Moses had led in the royal palace.

The passion of rachmones, bred into him at his mother's breast, had opened Moses to the plight of others, most poignantly towards those with whom he felt closest kinship. In slaying the Egyptian guard, he was renouncing his identification with royal society, thereby exercising as he never had before, an act of radical dissent. **Rachmones and dissent were the twin values in habiru life to which all else adhered. A perfect counterpart to the mandate of "benefits and obedience," rachmones and dissent lay at the heart of a newly emerging culture, one that would prove to be profoundly different from the social order that prevailed in its surroundings.** Moses felt good. He was finding his habiru self.

One thing led to another. Success in making war upon their oppressor led Moses to a desire for making peace among his people. *"And when he went out the second day, behold two men of the Hebrews strove together, and he said to him that did the wrong, Wherefore smitest thy fellow?"* The response he received was indelibly habiru. *"Who made thee a prince and a judge over us?"* I can still hear the question ringing in Jewish families today, and in partnership board rooms. With the best of intentions, Moses had still to be purged of the courtly arrogance in which he grew up.

There was more. *"Intendest thou to kill me,"* the wrong-doer cast in Moses face, *"as thou killedst the Egyptian?"* The captive grapevine is never idle, and the word was out. *"And Moses feared, and said, Surely this thing is known."* Though executions in Egypt were ordered strictly by the book, someone of royal blood might get away with one, not so a habiru. *"Now when Pharaoh heard this thing, he sought to slay Moses. But Moses fled from the face of Pharaoh, and dwelt in the land of Midian, and he sat down by a well."* [40] There, from Jethro the Midianite, Moses would receive valuable lessons in shared leadership, a fundamental necessity if ever he hoped to guide the habiru in ways with which they were familiar.

"This thing is too heavy for thee," Jethro would tell Moses, *"thou art not able to perform it thyself alone . . . Thou shalt provide out of*

all the people able men, such as fear God, men of truth, hating covetousness; and place such over them to be rulers of thousands, and rulers of hundreds, rulers of fifties, and rulers of tens. And let them judge the people at all seasons . . . and they shall bear the burden with thee." [41]

Far from the court of the pharaoh, a sheepherder and desert trader teaches Moses the secret of decentralized authority. Among the habiru, loosely organized in clans and families, widespread authority was the natural way of doing things. A nation of judges, when many lived without rulers, the era would be memorialized forever in the *Book of Judges*. Acquiring a coherence that had been inspired by Moses' own vision, the time of the judges must have seen a great flowering of habiru culture and society. It was destined to continue up until the inauguration of an Israelite monarchy. To this culture Moses would contribute an ingrained appreciation of order, instilled as he grew to maturity in pharaoh's house. Devoting order to a defense of dissent, however, rather than employing it to squelch dissident viewpoints was the skill he needed to master. Tricky, and he was never fully to grasp it, but then, who has?

All this lay in Moses' future. At the moment, however, his attention was focused in quite another direction. *"Now [Jethro] the priest of Midian had seven daughters, and they came and drew water, and filled the troughs to water their father's flock . And the shepherds came and drove them away, but Moses stood up and helped them, and watered their flock."* One might be inclined to regard this event as another instance in Moses' growing sense of both rachmones and dissent. If so, it would seem that other sentiments, quite natural in a young man, were also at work, and with predictable consequences. Then Jethro *"gave Moses Zipporah his daughter. And she bore him a son, and he called his name Gershom, for he said, I have been a stranger in a strange land."* [42]

Rachmones will reverberate distinctly and not altogether fortuitously in the passion of grokking with which Robert Heinlein graces his own "stranger in a strange land." The biblical use of the designation can be understood in various ways. Obviously at face value, it was an allusion to Moses' circumstances in the land of the Midianites. The land was strange to him and he was a stranger within it. Beyond that, however, as stateless citizens and wandering brigands, the habiru all were strangers to the lands around them, not only in a political sense but culturally as well. In return, the cultural land being cultivated by the habiru was indeed a strange anomaly amidst the Bronze-Age empires that encompassed the entire region.

Much of the appeal of Heinlein's tale can be ascribed to the widespread feeling that we are still "strangers in a strange land," [43] bearing within us the certainty that we've been made for something other than the life we know, carrying about a collaborative heritage that waits to be redeemed. Rachmones, grokking, Hawaiian *aloha,* South African Nguni *ubuntu,* most all peoples have their own name for it.

"Now Moses kept the flock of Jethro his father in law," for how many years we do not know, perhaps half a lifetime, during which a second son, Ezekiel - "El-is-my-help," was born. The contrast between the splendors of a royal court and the vast, empty stretches of semi-arid wasteland could hardly have been greater. Here there were no rules for Moses to follow, no facile courtesies to be extended or bendings of the knee before superiors.

One can only imagine the thoughts that passed through Moses' mind as day after day he had little but Jethro's sheep to keep him company. His successful assault upon the Egyptian guard may have inspired the realization that the military might of royal Egypt was not invincible. The entire aggregate of Egyptian gods and goddesses, in adulation of whom Moses had been so assiduously instructed, had not kept the guard from death. More disturbing was the habiru rejection of his efforts at making peace among them. How might people such as this rise to a sense of pride in themselves? Order was needed. Moses had learned the value of order in the royal court, not however the order he'd seen employed in the regimentation that pervaded Nilotic society, but rules of law that would safeguard the free spirit of the habiru.

And what of a god? A daring venture of great magnitude was taking shape in Moses' thoughts. Could it be embarked upon without divine sanctification? Not likely. Was there a god then to call upon? Those of Egypt were clearly out of the question. Ra, Horus and Osiris would be despised forever in memories of the oppression that the habiru had known in their names. Bel, Baal, Marduk, Molech and the other gods of the lands from which the habiru had fled were tainted by similar reputations. The habiru had suffered their fill under all of them. El, then, *I'lah* as he was known among some of the desert tribes, why not El? Most favored among the habiru, a number of towns had already sprung up in Canaan, Moses heard, taking the name of El, Joseph-El and Jacob-El among them. Hadn't he himself named his second son Ezekiel? Less devoted to mythic conquest and involved in divine intrigue, of all the gods El seemed most amenable to providing guidance for habiru society. Still in all, El too had acquired a history of partisanship. A god was needed who meted out justice impartially to all, whoever they were and from wherever they came.

All this and much else Moses must have mulled over during the heated days and bitterly cold nights that he spent alone in the desert. As would be the case with Jesus of Nazareth and Gautama Buddha, refining the temperament and clearing the psyche in solitude and wanderings, the heritage brooding inside Moses had ample space and time to mature into a glittering vision of deliverance.

The scribes assure us that the vision came upon Moses one day in the desert outback in the blaze of a burning bush. *"And the angel of the Lord appeared unto him in a flame of fire out of the midst of a bush, and he looked, and, behold, the bush burned with fire, and the bush was not consumed . . . And God called unto him out of the midst of the bush, and said, Moses, Moses. And he said, Here am I."* [44] So it may have been. Radiant glows are commonplace sights in trance states, under the influence of hallucinogenics and during meditation. There are visits by deities and spirits, voices that ring with the veracity of things actually heard. Fiery auras are seen. Whatever the circumstances were, the imagery of the burning bush suggests a signal experience of energized awareness. Moses had been seized by an inspiration of impelling grandeur.

"Now therefore, behold," Moses hears the voice of God tell him, *"the cry of the children of Israel is come unto me, and I have also seen the oppression wherewith the Egyptians oppress them. Come now therefore . . . bring forth my people the children of Israel out of Egypt."* [45]

In the midst of his exaltation, Moses was taken aback. Beneath the veneer of elitist insolence that he had picked up in the royal house, he was after all a rather unassuming person, not quite sure of himself in his relations with others, letting them do the talking. In later years this would be remembered. *"Now this man Moses was very meek, above all the men which were on the face of the earth."* [46] Although looked down upon by the powerful, meekness may be a covering over a reservoir of compelling strength. That the greatest strength of all proceeds from a heart of the most exquisite softness was a truth known from the very beginning to Chinese philosophy, and doubtless understood in some measure by peoples everywhere. Subject to an almost fanatic certainty of purpose, Moses' quality of "meekness" would serve him well in rallying the habiru to his vision. At the time however he was confused and doubtful.

"And Moses said unto God, Who am I . . . that I should bring forth the children of Israel out of Egypt? And he [God] *said, Certainly I will be with thee."* Allied with the power of the divine, Moses doubts were clearing. Still in all, how was he to convince the habiru? *"And Moses said unto God, Behold, when I come unto the children of Israel, and shall say unto them, The God of your fathers hath sent me unto you, and they shall say to me, What is his name? what shall I say unto them?"* The question was pivotal.

"And God said unto Moses, I AM THAT I AM, and he said, Thus shalt thou say unto the children of Israel, I AM hath sent me unto you." [47] Scholars have wrestled endlessly with the sense of this passage. To the habiru it could be instantly meaningful. Here in a moment of stunning clarity, the god of a dissident culture was proclaiming his independence of special privilege. No-one could claim him as his own, for he belonged to everyone. No figurehead for private authority, he was a god of sheer existence, at once both personal and universal.

Here was the revelation for which Moses had spent many long days alone in the desert. He had found a god who asked for nothing other than to be recognized for what he was, a god to whom the habiru could relate and call their own. In his name of I AM this was the god of free presence that every habiru felt in his heart. Other gods might be cast in bronze and clothed in gold, their towering images devoted to greed and dedicated to oppression. This god needed no images any more than he required a name. He was there to be what he was. The habiru could call him their own, and in his name that was no name recognize the strength that they themselves truly possessed. Around a god such as this, Moses was certain, the habiru could be rallied, firmly to lay hold of the life for which so many for so long had fought and died.

Moses' heart swelled. The vision burned within him, a fire that refused to be extinguished. Going before him always, it would lead him and the habiru back to Canaan, the land of promise which they had made their home, and from which so many had been carried away to slavery in Egypt. It would be a grand reunion, and a new beginning. Moses knew now what he needed to do. But how and when? Up and down the Nile and out into the desert stretches beyond, pharaoh's guards and armies swarmed over the land. With little else for weapons than staves and pitchforks, the habiru would be facing vast numbers of well-trained archers and chariots. Tending Jethro's sheep and caring for his family, Moses settled down to bide his time, sure in his heart that the right moment would come. He would leave matters in the laps of the gods, or rather, he thought, correcting himself, to the one god of his vision who had spoken to him with only the name of I AM.

He hadn't long to wait. Perhaps, it might be said, the same circumstances that prompted Moses' vision also brought about the possibility of its fulfillment. Caravans of traders passing by along the spice route soon brought tales of disaster and revolt that had befallen Egypt. *"Men sit in the bushes until the benighted traveler comes in order to plunder his burden, and what is upon him is taken away. He is belabored with blows of a stick and murdered . . . The washerman refuses to carry his load . . . The servant takes what he finds . . . Female slaves are free with their tongues."* This was far from being the Egypt that Moses fled. People knew their place then, and if they did not, they soon learned it. The meticulously enforced rules of conduct in relations between master and servant had slipped. There was brigandage on the roads.

Worse still for the fortunes of the state, *"Serving-men have become masters of butlers, and he who was once a messenger now sends someone else . . . He who had no loaf is now the owner of a barn, and his storehouse is provided with the goods of another . . . Behold, noble ladies are now on rafts . . . while he who could not sleep even on walls is now the possessor of a bed. Behold, the possessor of wealth now spends the night thirsty, while he who once begged his dregs for himself is now the possessor of overflowing bowls. Behold, the possessors of robes are now in rags, while he who could not weave for himself is now a possessor of fine linen . . . and the men of rank can no longer be distinguished from him who is nobody . . . Behold, he who had no yoke of oxen is now the owner of a herd . . . he who had no grain is now the owner of granaries . . . Indeed, gold and lapis lazuli, silver and turquoise, carnelian and amethyst . . . are strung on the necks of maidservants . . . Indeed, poor men have become owners of wealth, and he who could not make sandals for himself is now a possessor of riches . . . The corn of [royal] Egypt is now common property . . . Good things are [spread] throughout the land, [meanwhile noble] housewives say, 'Oh that we had something to eat!' . . . Indeed, noblemen are in distress, while the poor man is full of joy. Every town says, 'Let us suppress the powerful among us.'"*

Law and order, so Moses hears, seem totally to have broken down. *"Behold, no offices are in their right place, like a herd running at random without a herdsman . . . Indeed, public offices are opened and their inventories are taken away . . . The laws of the council chamber are thrown out . . . men walk on them in public places, and poor men break them up in the streets . . . The great council-chamber is a popular resort, and poor men come and go to the Great Mansions . . . The troops whom we marshaled for ourselves have turned into foreigners and have taken to ravaging . . . The king has been deposed by the rabble . . . The nomes are laid waste, and barbarians from abroad have come to Egypt."*

Under these conditions, the system of corporate acquisition and distribution, such as Joseph contrived for the pharaoh, was no longer functional. *"Indeed, the Nile overflows, yet none plough for it . . . The storehouse is empty and its keeper is stretched on the ground . . . Everywhere barley has perished . . . Neither fruit nor herbage can be found."* The consequences were inevitable. *"Pestilence is throughout the land, blood is everywhere . . . Indeed, many dead are buried in the river . . . The river is blood, yet men drink of it.*" [48]

Moses exulted. The Lord's call rang in his head. *"Go, return into Egypt, for all the men are dead which sought thy life."* Yes, he would return, bringing with him word of this new god, a god who would join the habiru to each other and to their ancestors in a way that was natural to them. It was a blessing, and Moses considered himself gifted in being so much a part of it. Bidding a farewell to Jethro, *"Moses took his wife and his sons and set them upon an ass, and returned to the land of Egypt."*

Along the way the family stops at an inn, and there Moses asks his wife to employ her medical expertise in performing an act that he considers to be of crucial importance. *"Then Zipporah took a sharp stone, and cut off the foreskin of her son, and cast it at his* [Moses'] *feet, and said, Surely a bloody husband thou art."* [49] Zipporah was horrified. Circumcision was a practice unknown to the Midianites. It was however a custom common among Western Semites generally, and they represented the preponderant presence among the habiru. Severing his son's foreskin, Moses was cutting himself off from the Egyptian society of his early years. He and his descendants would be irrevocably habiru.

▪

The elders were gathered around him, and beyond them as far into the darkness as Moses could see, a great throng of habiru. For weeks, having returned to Egypt, he'd been talking with the habiru, alone, in twos and threes, and in groups, disclosing something of his vision, hearing their response. They listened, many understood and approved. Expectations were ignited, there was excitement in the air. A sense of imminent destiny was taking hold in people's minds. Now, as they flocked to hear Moses speak, people wondered what might be decided.

Moses was ready. No stutter would impede his speech. These were his people. The "meekness" that one day would be legendary gave way to a quiet, unassuming certainty of purpose. In moments when his voice rose, it was with a passion of conviction rather than the harsh clamor of a harangue. Impelled by his vision, he felt assured of the outcome.

Moses had begun by recalling the freedom that the habiru once enjoyed. Now they were bondmen and slaves, while the families of those who had found wives lived in like servitude. "Obedient to the rules by which you are bound," Moses quietly went on in the midst of the hushed crowd, "and unflinching in the tasks that are set before you, you count yourself blessed in benefiting by a meager ration wherewith to stay alive, when even that much is given. Many fall, others are beaten down. Punishment is swift and delivered often for trivial lapses of attention to the duties that are assigned. Who among you can say his back shows no mark from the lash?" Murmurs of agreement from all sides, cries and curses.

"Even those of you who are fortunate enough to find service in homes of the rich labor in constant fear. This is not the life for which you have fought," Moses, now in a stronger voice, reminded the assemblage, "and in defense of which your fathers died and their fathers before them."

Moses paused. The pain and anger making its way through his audience was palpable. "Things are not good for Pharaoh," Moses continued. "Highwaymen wait in the dark and plunder the traveler. Bands of thieves roam the countryside, fighting each other and stealing grain from villagers. Judges desert their stations lest their lives be forfeit at the hands of those against whom they deliver judgment. Singing and dancing occupy the council chambers. Servants mock their masters. The rich are made poor, and the poor seize their possessions. Fields lie idle to the plough, and granaries are empty. People fall sick and die, and there is no-one to care for them.

The ranks of Pharaoh's armies are shredded through the flight of deserters."

As the crowd listened, Moses sensed impatience among them, a growing desire to act. "Knowing the weakness of Pharaoh's rule, many habiru have fled, some joining deserters from the army, others in the company of bondmen and slaves who were brought captive from the many countries that have been plundered by Egypt." Pausing to take a deep breath, Moses assessed the mood that his account had evoked. "Never in all the long years of our captivity," he went on, emphasizing each word, "have we enjoyed so propitious a moment in freeing ourselves from slavery in this land. Now is the time to act!"

A great shout went up. People rose to their feet and flung their fists in the air, each one complimenting his neighbor on doing the same. The entire throng, Moses felt, was poised for flight. His voice was now loud but calm. "We have it within our power to leave this accursed place. Freedom is within reach of our hands. The lands of our fathers wait for our return, and we are prepared to go." A deep hush had fallen over the assemblage. With their minds drawn to the edge of an exodus, thoughts flooded in of the things they would leave behind, and memories of the life to which they would come home. Moses waited. The moment had arrived for sharing his vision. His voice might shake in the words he went on to deliver, but he would never falter.

"I have had a vision," Moses began, speaking slowly now in measured tones, directing his voice to the very fringes of the assembly. "In my vision I saw the habiru return to the land from which you were plucked. As before, you came and went as you pleased. Each man judged for himself according to what seemed right to him. Sharing meals in high places, you held life with one another to be precious. Taking pride in your works, as of old, there was joy among you."

Utter silence, broken only by the chirping of crickets and here and there a subdued sigh. "Such is the life to which we will return," Moses continued, gently now, his words echoing the fullness in his heart. "All will be well with you, and you will live in peace. Ask yourselves however, How long then will you have that life?" The question was unexpected, a shudder ran through the crowd. "Now the Egyptians are weak. In my vision I saw them strong again, and coming down upon you once more like a lion in the fold. Other nations too I saw, some whose names today we scarcely know, Babylonians, Assyrians, Chaldaeans, Persians, Philistines, and others after them, each more rapacious than the one that came before. You will be carried off to many lands, those of you who are spared, so my vision went, your wives, your children, your goods." Moses' voice quavered. "I saw you torn among nations, scattered far and wide in strange places."

"How will you preserve the life for which so long and with such great courage you have fought?" Moses had come to the issue around which all else revolved. "You are not like those who live in the places from which you fled. You do not long to see the inside of palaces, nor covet slaves to do your bidding. You do not wag your tail for the master's bone, trading him vows of servitude that you might fill your belly. You are strangers to those others, they who live in greed and fear, strangers to their ways, and they are strangers to you. Fleeing from all the lands around, you have sought refuge in free places, where each has equal say and no man lords it over another. Wherever you may be taken captive or where you have fled, in that free spirit, held in common among brethren, you have your home."

He had touched a common chord, Moses knew, one that reverberated in his own heart. "How will the life we know and hold so dear be preserved? I asked this question, and in the midst of my confusion, a voice rang in my ears. 'The cry of my children,' it said, *'is come unto me, and I have also seen the oppression wherewith the Egyptians oppress them. Come now therefore . . . that thou mayest bring forth my people . . . out of Egypt.'* [50]

"So the voice began. Whose voice was it? I knew not, yet it went on. *'I will take you to me for a people, and I will be unto you a God, and ye shall know that I am the Lord your God.'* [51] In my vision I could contain myself no longer. Who then are you, I asked this voice, what is your name? *'I AM THAT I AM,'* the voice responded. *'Thus shalt you say . . . I AM hath sent me unto you.'*"

The crowd stirred uneasily. Cries of doubt mingled with those of derision. "Has he no name? What can we do with a god that has no name, and he with us? How can a god without a name lead us, look over us, minister to our needs? What kind of god is this that we might take him for our own?" The effect of his vision in peril, Moses had anticipated responses such as these. "What name then would you like your god to bear?" he inquired. "Ra, Osiris or Horus, Baal or Bel, bloody Anat or avaricious Molech who devours the bodies of children alive in his flames? They are the gods at whose hands you have suffered, and from whom you have fled. Greed and oppression are their lot, they rule through injustice." In the circle of elders heads were nodding in agreement. "What god do you know," Moses inquired of those who had come to listen, "who thinks as you think, feels what you feel, and acts in ways that you can call your own?"

The question hung heavily in the air. What before had seemed simple, now posed a problem, and the problem needed to be dealt with. "El!" one voice cried out at last, and others took up the refrain. "We will have El! El will be our god!" This too Moses was expecting. "El?" he reiterated as a question. "El, El!" voices rang out once again in response. "Yes, El," Moses went on, almost introspectively. "One day you may choose El for your god, or perhaps some other. That day is not yet come. Look to yourselves now only. Neither the hirelings of princes and kings nor the playthings of cruel gods, you are your own people. Unwilling to be what kings or gods would make of you, you have run from their states and their ways. You are habiru, citizens of a state that you hold in your hearts. You are what you are."

He was being heard now, Moses felt. "What god then can you have," he continued, "other than one, like yourselves, who is what he is, nothing else. Do you dispute against evil laws and unjust punishments, this god will be your support. His word even, you may question when you are displeased with it. He has no name because he belongs to everyone. And yet, just as you differ from the peoples around, it is you this god has chosen from all the others to be his own. So it was said to me in my vision: *'Ye shall be a peculiar treasure unto me above all people, for all the earth is mine . . . I will walk among you and will be your God, and ye shall be my people.'* [52] Wherever you may go, he will be with you. Nor ever will he forsake you, so long as you hold fast to all for which you have fought. This is the god who came to me in my vision, and I have embraced him." Moses leaned heavily upon his staff. He had said enough, perhaps more than he intended. Offering a vision so new, however, and unfamiliar, he'd felt impelled to make it clear as he could to those who had come to listen.

Waves of murmuring voices swept through the crowd. Slowly the sounds of discussion gave way to tones of approval. Moses waited for the voices to quiet down. At last someone asked, "What does this god wish us to do?" Others echoed the question. "Yes! Tell us!" The god of the habiru had been accepted. Refreshed in the knowledge that all would now go well, Moses responded. "This god asks nothing more of you than what you already are. In my vision he came to me as *'a God full of compassion, and gracious, long-suffering, and plenteous in mercy and truth.'* [53] Are these not the very words in which you would speak of all that is best in yourselves?"

Shouts of approval rang out through the night air. Had Moses' eyes been able to penetrate the dark, he would have seen streams of tears running down furrowed cheeks. "'Let them make their customs into laws then,' this god said to me, 'so that they may take pride in who they are, nor fade away in time and that others too may know.'"

Habiru customs had evolved over hundreds of years, and were familiar to all. Rendering them into laws required little more than stating the customs as they already existed. "Here then are the laws," Moses began, offering an injunction upon which, before all others, life in collaborative society must rest. "*Thou shalt not avenge, nor bear any grudge against the children of thy people, but thou shalt love thy neighbour as thyself.*" [54] From this it followed naturally that, "*Thou shalt not defraud thy neighbour, neither rob him. The wages of him that is hired shall not abide with thee all night until the morning.*" [55] And also, Moses continued, "*If thy brother be waxen poor, and fallen in decay with thee, then thou shalt relieve him, yea, though he be a stranger, or a sojourner, that he may live with thee. Take thou no usury of him, or increase.*" [56] Welfare without a state.

Short of parity in one's dealings with others, first of all in the economics of staying alive, brotherly love, valuable in itself, could hardly have counted as more than an ideal. Equality of persons could defer to no exceptions, neither among immigrants to the community nor even as regards visitors. "Strangers" and "sojourners," the laws would reiterate time and again, enjoyed common standing with everyone else in habiru society. If in later days, Jews would acquire an inhospitable notoriety as bankers and usurers, the heritage might well be traced so far back as the financial acumen of Joseph in Egypt.

A strange calm had settled over the crowd. Frequently given to argument and debate, now they sat as though entranced. Their life, the ways in which they had chosen to live, was being spread out before them. For the first time ever they were able to see themselves upon a screen larger than that visible through their local affairs with each other. They were awestruck, felt humbled as the familiar world of their daily lives unfolded into a vision with no discernible bounds. Lips silently moving, almost even as Moses would speak it, they knew what else was coming, startled in the knowledge of their own awareness.

"'Ye shall do no unrighteousness in judgment,'" Moses went on, *"'in meteyard, in weight, or in measure. Just balances, just weights, a just ephah [bushel], and a just [collection] bin, shall ye have.'"* [57] Equal trade at the weigh station, so often violated in the societies from which they had fled, was sanctified by the habiru in a parity of offerings before the divine. *"'The rich shall not give more, and the poor shall not give less than half a shekel, when they give an offering.'"* [58] The rich were denied the indulgence of parading the weight of their wealth in the presence of divinity, nor could the poor be shamed in a display of their poverty. When later the affluence of cattle herders overtook the modest holdings of dirt farmers, the Lord's preference for the offering of Abel would serve as a condemnation of Cain.

Aroused at last from the spell into which they had fallen, the audience now joined lustily in Moses' presentation. "Weights, measures and offerings," someone called out, "what about justice?" The question resonating with Moses' own thoughts, as though on cue, he renewed his recital of the laws that were to be adopted. *"'Thou shalt not wrest the judgment of thy poor in his cause.'"* [59] A great roar went up. Shouts of approval mingled with expressions of joy, as people congratulated themselves on having rejected the devices of injustice with which they were familiar before the seats of the mighty.

"'Ye shall do no unrighteousness in judgment. Thou shalt not respect the person of the poor, nor honour the person of the mighty, but in righteousness shalt thou judge thy neighbour.'" [58] How different, Moses thought, was this heritage from his life at the court of the Pharaoh, where the differential punishment of persons was written into law. His speech quickened. "And again," Moses said, expanding from one law to the next. He was laying the foundations, he had come to realize, of both a nation and its religion, and he was gripped by a feeling of awe. *"'Hear the causes between your brethren, and judge righteously between every man and his brother, and the*

stranger that is with him. Ye shall not respect persons in judgment, but ye shall hear the small as well as the great.'" [61] Finally, *"One law and one manner shall be for you . . . as well for the stranger as for one of your own country.'"* [62]

Embroiled in controversies over issues of granting rights to some while withholding them from others, America today has moved far from this simple rule of universal justice. Among the habiru the matter was clear. Virtually everyone present had known the gulf that existed between the laws enacted by royal despots and the way in which they were administered. Recognizing an equal standing in judgment for all in the land, whatever their station in life, ethnicity or origin, in ways quite unknown within the corporate societies of the day, habiru customs had bridged the gap that so often separated the law from the manner of its delivery.

Moses felt tired, suddenly assailed with weariness. His entire life had been involved in his vision. The enormity of the undertaking now hung heavily upon his shoulders. Images of the desert came to him, with its undemanding bleakness. He weaved unsteadily about his staff. The administration of justice was the keystone against which all else rested. Now Moses scarcely had the energy to raise it into place. The assemblage stirred uneasily.

At last, one among the elders stood up. Following Moses' own lead, he too spoke popular customs into the form of laws. *"Thou shalt not raise a false report,'"* the elder enjoined. *"Put not thine hand with the wicked to be an unrighteous witness.'"* [63] Nods of approval as the elder continued. *"But one witness shall not testify against any person to cause him to die* [64] *... At the mouth of two witnesses, or three witnesses, shall he that is worthy of death be put to death, but at the mouth of one witness he shall not be put to death. The hands of the witnesses shall be first upon him to put him to death, and afterward the hands of all the people.'"* [65]

No matter how serious the alleged transgression, the habiru felt, a man's life cannot rest on the testimony of a single witness. It was their practice, moreover, to assure that anyone who accuses someone else of having transgressed, must also take responsibility for initiating the punishment. And then, the entire community as well needed to participate. A crime against one was a crime against all. Their attachment to life, and a determination to preserve it freely as it should be lived, had driven the habiru from the precincts of those who contrived to bend life to their own purposes. Life was valued. Taking it from a man was no small matter.

"*There shall be six cities for refuge,*" rising to his feet, a second elder announced, "*which ye shall appoint for the manslayer, that he may flee thither . . . That the manslayer die not, until he stand before the congregation in judgment*" Not a chief, not even a judge, could deliver a verdict in the case of a homicide, only the congregation as a whole. "*These six cities shall be a refuge both for the children of Israel and for the stranger, and for the sojourner among them, that every one that killeth any person unawares may flee thither.*' And if the congregation shall judge the slaying to have been without intent," the elder concluded, "then, '*the congregation shall deliver the slayer out of the hand of the revenger of blood, and the congregation shall restore him to the duty of his refuge, whither he has fled.*'" [66] The right to sanctuary was declared, and, one after another, six voices called out, "Rezer, Ramoth, Golan, Kedesh, Shechem, Kirjath-arba," each of them the name of a city that had so served.

The just delivery of justice, upon which the habiru so zealously insisted, had been made into law. Moses exulted. The worst of his failings, he had been advised on more than one occasion, was his tendency to dominate with an overpowering sense of righteousness. Others, Moses now plainly saw, were equally capable. Their intervention had given him time to restore the fire in his vision. Reinvigorated, Moses next turned to the vexing problem of servitude. Themselves refugees from bondage, the habiru had evolved a variety of ways to ameliorate the relations between master and servant. These too would now become law.

   "'Thou shalt not oppress an hired servant that is poor and needy,'" Moses began in a general way, *"'whether he be of thy brethren, or of thy strangers that are in thy land within thy gates. At his day thou shalt give him his hire, neither shall the sun go down upon it, for he is poor, and setteth his heart upon it, lest he cry against thee unto the Lord, and it be sin unto thee.'"* [67] The Lord might not happen to be listening, but the ears of the entire community would be open to a poor man wailing over the deprivation of his wages. Not many in royal society would care to hear, the habiru knew from bitter experience, if even the cheated laborer dared voice his grievance.

   Respect for labor was evidently so integral to habiru life that alone among all western peoples, they observed a weekly day of rest. Moses now formulated this day into a law, applying it to all whatever their calling in life. *"But the seventh day is the sabbath of the Lord thy God. In it thou shalt not do any work, thou, nor thy son, nor thy daughter, thy manservant, nor thy maidservant, nor thy cattle, nor thy stranger that is within thy gates.'"* [68] Based heavily as they were on slave labor and indentured service, a day of rest for those who worked was scarcely considered in corporate societies. During the centuries preceding Jesus, the law of the holy day of rest earned the God of Moses' vision more than a few converts.

   If it was truly to be upheld, the sanctity of life could not end at the doorstep of one's own dwelling. Even though a royal adoptee, Moses recalled, his habiru origins made him a convenient butt of insults and derision, behavior that habiru considered intolerable in their own company. How much worse was the lot of servants and slaves, whose mutilation in the societies around them was deemed to be hardly a matter of concern. The habiru saw things differently. Servants and bondsmen were to be treated with the same measure of respect as anyone else, and the community held their masters accountable.

  "'And if a man smite the eye of his servant,'" Moses lays out, his voice impassioned in memories of personal outrage, *"'or the eye of his maid, that it perish, he shall let him go free for his eye's sake. And if he smite out his manservant's tooth, or his maidservant's tooth, he shall let him go free for his tooth's sake.'"* [69] Hearing these words, expressions of scorn might well have creased the faces of those who had served in the households of Babylon, Ur, Nippur or any other of the cities along the two rivers. A servant or slave was regarded there, one could read it in the Code of Hammurabi, as little other than an economic asset. Liabilities for maiming or slaying a slave were levied only if the slave belonged to someone else, as compensation for damaged goods.

  With relish Moses now introduced the custom of the Jubilee. In this practice in particular he felt reflected most profoundly what it meant to be a habiru. *"Then shalt thou cause the trumpet of the jubile to sound on the tenth day of the seventh month. In the day of atonement shall ye make the trumpet sound throughout all your land."* The habiru Jubilee took its name from the *yobhel*, the ram's horn whose call was trumpeted on that occasion. [70] *"The poor shall never cease out of the land,"* Moses intoned slowly and with emphasis, as though he himself had become the yobhel. *"Therefore . . . thou shalt open thine hand wide unto thy brother, to the poor, and to thy needy in thy land. And if thy brother, an Hebrew man, or an Hebrew woman, be sold unto thee, and serve thee six years then in the seventh year thou shalt let him go free from thee. And when thou sendest him out free from thee, thou shalt not let him go away empty. Thou shalt furnish him liberally out of thy flock, and out of thy floor, and out of thy winepress.'"* [71] Fields that had been contracted out were also to be restored to their original owners.

There are few words in the English language that resound with such connotations of joy as are evoked in "jubilation." Like the sound of the yobhel, it calls out a message of freedom in its purest sense. Spread on the wings of longing, through sermons, songs and shouts the diaspora of an idea has reached even into those hearts that are hardened against its authors. Under the impact of affluence and monarchy, no doubt at the insistence of major stakeholders in the economy, the years of the Jubilee were later extended from seven to forty-nine. The spirit of liberation in which it was conceived would survive forever.

Among the habiru, traffic in human beings was altogether out of the question. Enslaving or selling someone into bondage was absolutely interdicted, and was punishable by death. "'And he that stealeth a man, and selleth him, or if he be found in his hand, he shall surely be put to death.'" [72] Once again, a roar of approval from the crowd. Life was worth little if not free.

"'Thou shalt not deliver unto his master the servant which is escaped from his master unto thee.'" Moses took a deep breath. There was hardly anything in habiru society that distinguished it more radically from that of its neighbors than the treatment that the habiru accorded to runaway slaves. Slave labor and bondage contracts were the live capital that sustained the fortunes of corporate empires. "If a citizen has harbored in his house either a fugitive slave male or female belonging to the state or to a private citizen" the Code of Hammurabi declares, "and has not brought him forth at the summons of the police, that householder shall be put to death." Runaway slaves were tortured and mutilated, slain and impaled. When apprehended, the kindliest fate a runaway slave could expect was to be bound into fresh servitude.

Runaways themselves, the habiru appreciated the plight of the runaway. Their society as a whole was a runaway society. The runaway deserved protection. "'He shall dwell with thee, even among *you, in that place which he shall choose in one of thy gates where it liketh him best. Thou shalt not oppress him.'"* [73] In evaluating the significance of this habiru custom, one has but to consider how runaway slaves were still being treated at late as 1865, three thousand years later, in the United States of America. The last stop on the Underground Railroad was Canada.

As something of a break from weightier considerations, Moses then introduced as laws practices that were commonly observed among the habiru as regards gleaning rights in cultivated fields. *"'When thou beatest thine olive tree, thou shalt not go over the boughs again. It shall be for the stranger, for the fatherless, and for the widow.* [74] ··· *And when ye reap the harvest of your land, thou shalt not wholly reap the corners of thy field, neither shalt thou gather the gleanings of the harvest. And thou shalt not glean thy vineyard, neither shalt thou gather every grape of thy vineyard. Thou shalt leave them for the poor and the stranger.'"* [75] No individual interest weighed heavier than the welfare of the community as a whole. People in need weakened the strength upon which a collaboratively oriented society relied. Providing for them out of the gleanings of olives, grapes and grain was generally regarded as a small enough matter. In 1857 Jean François Millet would paint *The Gleaners*, gracing French humanism with an unforgettable image. The habiru assembly adopted the law without comment.

Nor was there any quarrel with the prohibition against employing a scorched earth policy for strategic purposes during combat. *"'When thou shalt besiege a city a long time, in making war against it, to take it, thou shalt not destroy the trees thereof by forcing an ax against them . . . for the tree of the field is man's life.'"* [76] One has only to read the ferocious accounts of destruction left behind by royal dynasts, and ascribed in the bible to Joshua himself, to appreciate the significance of a law that reflected little else than the exercise of common sense in the preservation of one's habitat.

In his exposition of the laws of the habiru, Moses was nearing the end. This then seemed a fitting moment to remind everyone of the circumstances under which they had come together. The stranger was to be specially honored. "*Thou shalt neither vex a stranger nor oppress him, for ye were strangers in the land of Egypt* [77] ··· *Also thou shalt not oppress the stranger, for ye know the heart of a stranger, seeing ye were strangers in the land of Egypt* [78] ··· *And if a stranger sojourn with thee in your land, ye shall not vex him. But the stranger that dwelleth with you shall be unto you as one born among you, and thou shalt love him as thyself, for ye were strangers in the land of Egypt.*" [79]

In these passages as in others, the bible speaks of the Israelites as having been strangers solely in Egypt. This is very much in keeping with the intent of the priestly scribes in mythifying the events of the Exodus while ignoring the early history of the habiru. Nevertheless, mention of the Israelites as having been strangers appears with surprising frequency throughout the canonical literature. In truth, outside of the homes that they eventually made for themselves in Canaan and adjacent lands, the habiru were strangers wherever they went. They had originated as strangers to the many lands from which they had come, this is the way they thought of themselves, and they welcomed others who joined them in the same spirit.

One matter only remained. This had to do with the treatment of women who were taken in war, and of this a number of elders had strongly advised Moses not to speak. Most habiru tribes and clans pursued a policy in this regard that Moses himself strongly endorsed. Others however vehemently objected to it. As a matter of integrity in fulfilling the entire spirit of the law, Moses decided to include it. "*When thou goest forth to war,*'" he therefore began, "*and seest among the captives a beautiful woman, and hast a desire unto her, that thou wouldest have her to thy wife, then thou shalt bring her home to thine house . . . And she shall put the raiment of her captivity from off her, and shall remain in thy house, and bewail her father and her mother a full month, and after that thou shalt go in unto her, and be her husband, and she shall be thy wife. And it shall be, If thou have no delight in her, then thou shalt let her go whither she will, but thou shalt not sell her at all for money, thou shalt not make merchandise of her, because thou hast humbled her.'"* [80]

A deathly silence descended over the throng. People sensed an imminent conflict to be brewing, as indeed it was. Arguments arose on all sides, and these rapidly heated up. The hour was late, people were groggy, inclined to be short-tempered, and dispute soon turned into scuffling and fighting as opposing points of view confronted each other with equal vigor. The treatment of women still haunted the habiru as an issue to which they had hardly yet come to terms. The customs that Moses now cited as laws were far in advance of any others of their time, and not surprisingly therefore too extreme for some of the habiru themselves. In so heavily based a warrior culture, despite its democratic emphasis, the delicacy of sentiment implied in this statute was perhaps greater than many men were able to embrace. In a state of near exhaustion himself, along with the handful of women present at the assemblage, Moses could do little but stand back and watch as shouts and blows erupted.

Shoulders sagging, Moses' gaze wandered off into space. The last words of the voice he had heard in his desert vision came back to him. *"Thou shalt have no other gods before me,"* the voice had proclaimed. *"Thou shalt not make unto thee any graven image, or any likeness of anything that is in heaven above, or that is in the earth beneath, or that is in the water under the earth. Thou shalt not bow down thy self to them, nor serve them."* And finally, *"Thou shalt not take the name of the Lord thy God in vain."* [81]

This god I AM was to be the only god. There were to be no others, and no images were to be fabricated in his worship. No-one, neither chief nor ordinary householder could claim to be speaking for him. In a single broad stroke, the voice that Moses heard had swept away the prerogative of kings and priests to attach god's will to their actions, along with the images wherewith they sought to beguile worshippers into accepting their authority. This god would be at the side of people, perhaps even within them, Moses gave it a thought, never however as a foil for their personal ambitions.

In the midst of the controversy still swirling about him, Moses felt a new confidence. This was the message he had to deliver. All that came before had been derived from habiru customs, and was familiar. A god who rejected all other gods, who renounced images and idolatry was new. He had appeared to Moses in his vision, and Moses was certain he was needed. In refusing other gods and even images of himself, and shutting himself off from those who would hawk their message in his name, this god declared all to be equal before him. He was habiru, and in him the habiru would see, as in a mirror, their own spirit. This god would be a haven for them, to which in time of fear and doubt they could return and be welcomed.

The tumult subsiding, Moses pounded the ground before him with his staff, and swept his arm across the heads of the throng in a plea for quiet. "I have one thing else to say before you," he told the assemblage. "One last thing that I heard in my vision from the god who has chosen you even before you chose him." And Moses relayed to people the commandments regarding his worship that the voice of the god had delivered to him. "This is the god who will be with you on your way out of Egypt," he concluded. "You are made in his image, as he is in yours."

The throng listened and wondered at the newness of what they were hearing. This god seemed right to them, most thought. Others were startled by the strangeness of it. No-one ventured to object, however, and Moses accepted this as indicating their assent. Truth is, people were fatigued with lack of sleep and the intensity of the event, and they were beginning to wander off, back to the settlements, homes and encampments from which they had come to attend the meeting. Much had happened, bringing them to look upon themselves in ways they had little considered before. Infused with new warmth in their regard for each other, tired little jokes passed among them as they walked away, each to his own destination. Looking closely, one might detect a sense of purpose and added sturdiness in the way they held themselves. That night they had become a new people, and, one way or another, everyone felt it.

How many genuinely had absorbed the message of the god they were now prepared to call their own was not all that clear. Indeed, people would soon enough be worshipping foreign gods alongside this one. There would be images. Aaron himself, first of the high priests, would initiate the worship of a golden calf. Winged cherubim, very much in the manner of the sacerdotal creatures that monarchs erected from Turkey to the Nile, would stand guard within the Ark of the Tabernacle around the throne of God. Prophets would broadcast their pronouncements as though in the breath of God's word. The god that Moses had presented to the habiru, despite his consonance with their own ways, was an ideal, not readily to be grasped. Still in all, in time, the spirit of the habiru would find a fitting home in that god, and there it would stay alive forever.

Elders and others who wished to work out the details of their exodus had stayed behind, and gathered quietly around Moses. Strategies were proposed, considered and a consensus arrived at. The time for the exodus from Egypt would be made known through messengers and by signal fires. Above the desert horizon, the glow of a new day was lofting into the eastern sky. Like a beacon of hope, Venus' last sparkle was all that remained of the stars. Moses felt his work was done. In reality, it had only just barely begun.

*

There is no account of Moses' speech to be found in the bible. In its place one hears of an epic conflict being conducted between the Lord and Pharaoh, with Moses and his brother Aaron serving principally as intermediaries. The devout may believe what they will. Cultures come whole into the world no more readily than species, however, especially so unique a culture as that of the habiru. In accepting as valid the biblical assertion that Hebrew society, culture and the laws issued fully formed from the hand of God, those who do so fall subject to practices of anthropological creationism. Differing hardly at all from the position taken by biological creationists, the viewpoint likewise contributes little if anything to the repository of awareness upon which the survival of all depends.

Realistically appraised, there is no way that a major undertaking such as the exodus could have occurred without deliberations of some sort. Within those deliberations, to judge by the honor accorded him in the scribal accounts, Moses must have played an instrumental role. I've endeavored to explore how that role might have unfolded. In doing so, I've deleted the many instances in which the laws are ascribed to the word of God. Nor have I dealt with the complex rituals of worship inserted by the scribes in what might otherwise have been a straightforward historical account. I've ignored as well the punitive measures that were directed against infractions of codes of behavior that today we would judge as being backward and repressive.

Less than admirable customs were undoubtedly present in habiru society, and not merely as an invention of the scribes. How much of it, however, is to be assigned to habiru times and how much to life under the monarchy that succeeded that era is an open question. At any rate, in passing by the less than decorous aspects of habiru life, it has not been my intention to deny their reality, rather to focus upon the extraordinary society that the habiru evolved from a combination of rachmones and dissent, and that was perpetuated through the vision of a remarkable man.

The bible depicts Moses as having been a vehicle of God. In the scenario evolved by the priestly scribes, God comes to Moses and chooses him to do his work. *"I will be with thy mouth, and teach thee what thou shalt say . . . and will teach you what ye shall do."* [82] From one point of view, one can hardly fault the scribes from magnifying the power of a god whose uniqueness was not being easily accepted. Nevertheless, with Hebrew culture arriving as a mandate from God, the priesthood could readily claim indispensability in supervising his worship.

The truth is likely to be very much the other way around. The priestly scribes acknowledge Moses as having been a lawgiver, albeit delivering laws that came from God. Candidly regarded, the laws that Moses presented to the habiru could only have emerged from their own customs. It was Moses' genius to weave those customs into the making of a culture. God, not Moses, was the instrument to be employed in realizing this endeavor. In a blazing vision, Moses had discovered a god fashioned in an image that was compatible with habiru society. As certainly as Jesus of Nazareth, Gautama Buddha, Muhammed and Zarathustra, Moses had created a new religion.

With the fleeting exception of Akhenaton, the magnitude of his achievement is all the more astonishing in realizing that Moses preceded the other grand figures of religious and philosophical innovation, Plato and Lao-tzu included, by at least half a millennium. Habiru customs at his back, it was Moses who first penetrated the confines of the dynastic imperative. It remained to be seen how this heritage would fare under the impact of Judean monarchy.

V Servants and Prophets

Every few weeks, Mr. Farber the eggman would visit us in our third-floor, East Bronx apartment. He delivered eggs and collected premiums for Workmen's Circle life insurance policies. Organized at the time in lodges that were rooted in the cities and shtetels from which Jews had immigrated to the New World, the Workmen's Circle describes itself as being a "membership-based, secular progressive community and cultural center." Started in 1892 by a group of cloakmakers in New York's Lower East Side, it aimed for a "fusion of socialist vision with Jewish cultural survival." [83]

I mention all this only in offering a proper context for the appreciation of a conversation that transpired one day when Mr. Farber came by. I must have been sixteen or seventeen years old at the time, and I happened to be present. Eggs safely stored in the ice box, and the few pennies that were required handed over for the monthly insurance premium, Mr. Farber sat down with my grandmother around the white, enamel-top kitchen table to exchange gossip and compare views on events of the day. On this occasion, for what reason I don't recall, Mr. Farber asked, "What do you think of religion?" In Yiddish, *"Vos denkt dir?"* - What do you think?

My grandmother was serving tea. A cube of sugar artfully nestled beneath her tongue as a measure of frugality, she was sipping her tea from a saucer. Pondering Mr. Farber's question, removing the sugar and laying it carefully on the lip of the saucer, at length, my grandmother responded. "Religion is an old man, a *yeshive bocher*" - a biblical scholar, she began, gazing contemplatively ahead with, I think, a slight smile of amusement playing around the corners of her mouth. "He has a long beard, and he sits sipping soup from a saucer.

There are lice in his beard, and as he drinks, his beard hangs down into the soup." [84]

With my halting mastery of Yiddish, I may have missed something in this interchange. The memory of what I caught, however, has remained firmly etched in my mind. Clothed in worn and faded black, his head bent forward to drink, his long grey beard trailing into the soup before him, the image of the yeshive bocher has remained immutably fixed in my memory. My grandmother's response to Mr. Farber was an apt metaphor for the failings of religious devotion. Better than any formal reasoning that occurred to me over the years, that vivid image of a bent back and a grey beard trailing through a saucer of soup served me as a certainty of the failure of religion itself. Before leaving, Mr. Farber took me aside confidentially to explain that socialism and insurance policies were not incompatible.

My grandmother came from a rural town not far from Warsaw. Siedlice, it was represented by its own chapter in the Workmen's Circle. With plainspeaking ways that gave way from time to time to insightful snippets of wisdom, I've always thought of my grandmother in terms of the peasant background that I assumed for her. Of a bitter person she'd say: "He's eating himself up alive." The etiology of cancer could hardly be better described.

She had two favorite songs, and I loved to hear my grandmother sing them. Whenever she chose to entertain company with stories about the Old Country, one was sure to be serenaded with the strains of *"Ay, ay, ay, bulblichke."* Hearing the word as *bublichke,* shy of its initial letter "l," the melody of it being so lovely, and her way of singing the song so filled with endearment, for years I thought of it as being a song about a sweet, little grandmother, one like my own. With her in mind, I myself still sing the opening line with loving passion.

My notion of what the song referred to was reinforced by my grandmother's favorite joke. It had to do with the *kamenyi bobbe*, the "stone grandmothers" that Tartar princes left in their wake all across the Siberian steppes. Intended as monuments to their heroism, in the absence of appropriately skilled carvers, with stubby bodies and chubby heads, these representations of the princes gave the appearance of a long line of old peasant women. My grandmother would laugh and laugh as she explained this. The joke was on the princes and on my grandmother herself, and in that unlikely confluence the mighty were taken down and the lowly accepted as they were. [85]

Bobbe and *buhbe* happen also to have been Yiddish words for grandmother, and *bobbitshke* signified a "darling little grandma." Then too, there was the *bobushke*, a head scarf worn by women, more generally first generation immigrants who in my time were customarily grandmothers. With so much to substantiate my understanding of the word I heard my grandmother sing, it was many years before I learned that I had been singing out my heart to a baked potato, the sort that was sold from ovens in the street on cold, wintry days. Polish winters being severe and peasant purses light, for little more than a hundredth of a zloty one might bring joy to one's insides. No wonder the tune was so lovely. The song my grandmother sang sends forth a longing for a "dear, little baked potato." Is that asking for too much?

My grandmother's other favorite song was equally beautiful, and its meaning was never in doubt. *"Uf 'em pripichuk,"* she would sing, On the stove - a pripichuk having a wide, overhanging shelf, *"es brent a fayerel,"* a small fire is burning, *"in der shtif iz heys,"* it's warm in the house, *"dort zetst a rebbele,"* a dear rabbi is sitting there, *"mit kleyner kinderlach,"* with little children - perched for warmth, my grandmother would explain, atop the pripichuk shelf, *"lernen alef beth,"* learning their ABCs. The song goes on, as the rabbi enjoins the children to recite after him. [86]

At the age of eight, I was housebound with a series of childhood illnesses. For months, my grandmother, not yet living with us, would come over almost daily to care for me while my mother was at work. She always brought along a copy of *Der Tag* - The Day, the less politicized of the two Yiddish papers that prominently circulated in New York. When she finished reading, my grandmother passed the paper on to me. Sitting on the floor beside my bed, I flipped through the pages, first surveying the bold print headlines, and then lingering over the lettering that accompanied the large cartoon on the editorial page. I hadn't the slightest inkling of what these Hebraic letters meant, but they fascinated me.

Big Little books had by this time become my constant companions. A hundred times over I turned the pages to relive the adventures of Little Orphan Annie, Dick Tracy and, my personal favorite, Buck Rogers in the 25th Century. I had therefore by this time grown familiar with tautly simplistic English lettering. By contrast, the Hebraic letters seemed wondrous. Great, bulging curves met my gaze, accompanied by soaring pennants and majestic folds. Little as I comprehended its meaning, a world of substance floated before my eyes, and I was entranced. Carefully cutting out the editorial cartoon of the day, I stored them all away. I wish I still had them.

Baked potatoes and learning, sustenance and intellect, were the twin focuses around which much of Jewish life revolved, at least in the working class families with whose sons I chummed. However poor our circumstances, ice boxes, and soon enough, Frigidaires, were always fully stocked. It never ceased to surprise me, visiting the homes of more affluent friends, to discover near empty refrigerators in the company of expensive furniture. The highest callings, our parents insisted, and zealously drilled into us were those of doctors, lawyers and, well, engineers. Rabbis were not mentioned. I realize now that these occupations mattered not only for the substantial income and respect that they brought, but that they counted equally well in nurturing one's intellect.

Jewish emphasis on intellectual achievement, it seems reasonably certain, is directly traceable to the spirit of dissent in which habiru society emerged. Rejection of the basic premises upon which surrounding peoples led their lives, driven as they were by assiduously inculcated mythic justification, was in itself no small feat of intellect. Survival of the disaffected society of the habiru demanded a continuous exercise of intelligence. In a world where deceit was the ordinary medium through which royal control was maintained, nothing could be taken at face value.

Others may look for the silver lining in the cloud, Jews are more than likely to search out the cloud within the silver lining. *"Even in laughter the heart is sorrowful, and the end of that mirth is heaviness,"* one is reminded in *Proverbs.* [87] The clouds are almost sure to be there, and acceptance of their reality has done much to sustain the survival of a dissident culture. Ten Jews, eleven opinions, in one of its many variations, the saying is often heard. With so much to think about, one had always to think for oneself. As a survival strategy, dissent thus yielded a standing order of skepticism, one that eventually drew Sigmund Freud into the unfamiliar realms of the unconscious, Albert Einstein into a vision beyond the limits of Newtonian physics, and Karl Marx into a repudiation of the entire economic system.

Notwithstanding the emphasis on intellect that became so integral a part of my life, after all these years it seems to me that the lessons I learned through my grandmother's songs, and the stories that she told, have far more to do with my Jewishness than anything else. The tone of her voice, her bearing, always so softly present, the way that she laughed at the absurd and sighed over the inevitable, passed the heritage of the habiru into my tissues and thoughts far more effectively than all the many books that I've read on the subject, or through my endless hours of cogitation over their meaning. Reflected in the splendid calligraphy of Hebraic letters, my grandmother's heritage slipped inside my heart. Religious instruction and ritual observance had never been part of my life. Their place in the absorption of my heritage was taken by my grandmother's stories and songs, and in the Hebrew letters that held the breath of rachmones in their full and graceful curves.

In the centuries that were to follow the Exodus and then the time of the judges, much that the habiru had molded into a culture would fall away under the impact of monarchy and the rule of a Jewish elite. However much assailed and compromised, however, the spirit of habiru rachmones and dissent, fanatically at times defended, would nevertheless live on. It was this spirit that I was blessed to acquire in the nuances of my grandmother's words and ways.

●

"In those days there was no king in Israel. Every man did that which was right in his own eyes." [88] So ends the *Book of Judges*, reiterating the statement for a second time. How long the time of the judges lasted we don't know. The biblical account attests the era as extending from the arrival of the survivors of the Exodus up until the inauguration of the first king of Israel. Since we cannot date the Exodus with certainty, we have no idea how long this period may have extended. Several centuries at least, we may infer, and safely assume that much the same state of affairs existed for some time prior to the Exodus.

If ever there were a golden age of habiru society, the Time of the Judges, and the years preceding, would have been it. The authors of the Epic of Creation, might well have regarded this state of affairs as a resurgence of "Chaos," to be quartered, bled, and fashioned into a more properly ordered society, implemented through the divine intervention of a warrior-king. Guided by the inspired vision of Moses, the habiru created their own order, manifesting their remarkable culture in a unique body of law, one that distinguished its people from all others of the day. Under those laws, with the assistance of judges whom they themselves appointed, the congregation ruled itself. It is to these years that we may assign the passage of habiru customs into a vigorous ethnic awareness. Impervious to oppression and decimation, it would persist virtually intact down to our own day, impacting upon world culture to a degree far outweighing the numbers of those in whom it has been preserved.

The Code of Hammurabi introduced a legacy of contractual legality into Western society. The laws of the habiru, by contrast, even as pared down by scribes to the Ten Commandments, have contributed a standard of humanitarianism to which all western peoples since have cleaved.

The bible tells us nothing of this culture except to cite the names of a succession of judges, including in their number both Deborah and Samson. We hear instead of virtually continuous combat, Israelites against neighboring peoples and amongst themselves. At one point, the Benjaminites are nearly exterminated by their fellow Israelites. Confining their attentions to the acts of warring factions and peoples, the scribes may very well be preparing the reader for a solution in the form of monarchy, willed of course by God. They had little incentive, it seems, to accredit anything resembling social order to the years that had not yet benefitted by the authority of kings and the services of a high priesthood.

We do learn from the bible in ample detail the frequency with which people deserted the God that Moses had introduced. Since ever the moment when Aaron poured the molten image of the Golden Calf, people, rulers and priests alike regularly submitted their hopes and prayers to one or another of the gods and goddesses who were worshipped in the lands thereabout. *"And the children of Israel,"* we read in one of a multitude of similar citations, *" . . . set themselves up images and groves in every high hill, and under every green tree."* [89] It seems that Moses' God counted for far less in perpetuating the society of the habiru than did their customs and his laws. It was only towards the days of the Maccabees that a firm appreciation of the One God superseded all others in people's minds.

The time of the judges ended abruptly.

"Then all the elders of Israel gathered themselves together, and came to Samuel unto Ramah. And said unto him . . . Now make us a king to judge us like all the nations . . . That we also may be like all the nations, and that our king may judge us, and go out before us, and fight our battles." [90] We may well imagine the identity of those so eager to be living under a monarchy, heads, no doubt, of greater and lesser corporate houses. In the event of invasion by a foreign power, the poor could scramble to the hills. The affluent needed to stand by their holdings. During the '50s, a similar argument was employed in support of Stalinism. With capitalist enemies on all sides waiting to pounce, the Soviet Union could only be preserved, so it was said, under conditions of dictatorial control.

Considering the nature of social consciousness that has prevailed since the inception of the Bronze Age, only two options would appear to be available for the preservation of a culture. Either surround oneself with a protective perimeter, maintained by a national state, or learn to survive in the interstices of the states within which one lives. The latter strategy is automatically adopted by peoples whose lands have been conquered by others. In the absence of a deeply seeded tradition of dissent, in the long run it is unfortunately almost certain to fail. And so, willy-nilly, people are likely to respond to domination by foreign nations with nationalist aspirations of their own.

Were people to live under the kingship that they were demanding, Samuel the seer, later to be accounted a prophet, was painfully aware of what would be coming.

"And he said, This will be the manner of the king that shall reign over you: He will take your sons, and appoint them for himself, for his chariots, and to be his horsemen, and some shall run before his chariots. And he will appoint him captains over thousands, and captains over fifties, and will set them to plow his ground, and to reap his harvest, and to make his instruments of war, and instruments of his chariots.

"And he will take your fields, and your vineyards, and your olive yards, even the best of them, and give them to his servants. And he will take the tenth of your seed, and of your vineyards, and give to his officers and to his servants. And he will take your menservants, and your maidservants, and your goodliest young men, and your asses, and put them to his work. He will take the tenth of your sheep, and ye shall be his servants." [91]

Little is wanting in this description, identical to the measures taken by royal houses everywhere in Bronze-Age society for the sake of ramifying their corporate interests. Things would be no different in a royally structured Israelite state than they were in the lands from which the habiru had fled. Not even royal benevolence could alter those consequences. As things turned out, there would be little more benevolence evident in the kingdoms of Judah and Israel than was extended to the populace by rulers elsewhere, and just as much corruption. Inevitably, as part of the bargain, religion would be transformed into an organ of the state.

"And ye shall cry out in that day," Samuel predicts, *"because of your king which ye shall have chosen you, and the Lord will not hear you on that day . . . Nevertheless the people refused to obey the voice of Samuel, and they said, Nay, but we will have a king over us."* [92]

Seeking out Samuel in one of the "high places" where people gathered to share a meal and give thanks, Saul the Benjaminite comes to the seer to be anointed first king of the Israelites. Cognizant of the inevitable, in a scene that is gratuitously effaced by scribal mystique, the sad-eyed seer complies. *"And the spirit of the Lord will come upon thee,"* Samuel promises Saul, *"and thou . . . shall be turned into another man."* One will hear of a second Saul, a thousand years later, on the road to Damascus, "turned into another man." Whether in assuming the role of monarch or missionary, with equal certainty one is likely to be turned away from oneself. It goes with the job. *"And all the people shouted, and said, God save the king."* [93] The year was 1020 b.c., or thereabouts.

Not everyone was pleased. When soon thereafter in his first royal edict Saul mobilizes the Israelites for a military confrontation with the Ammonites, people balk. *"And the people said unto Samuel, Who is he who said, Shall Saul reign over us? Bring the men, that we may put them to death."* [94] Himself having been the source of Saul's investiture, the prophet assures everyone that with God on their side no-one will die. The rebellion is quelled.

The spirit of rebellion against authority had surfaced many years earlier. Fresh out of Egypt and still in the wilderness, the journey of Exodus is interrupted by a protest. *"And they rose up before Moses, with certain of the children of Israel, two hundred and fifty princes of the assembly, famous in the congregation, men of renown. And they gathered themselves together against Moses and against Aaron, and said unto them, Ye take too much upon you, seeing all the congregation are holy, every one of them, and the Lord is among them. Wherefore then lift ye up yourselves above the congregation of the Lord?"* [95] In sanctifying the egalitarianism which figured so prominently in habiru customs, the protesters were exhibiting a lively esteem of the God that Moses himself had given them.

Moses calls upon leaders of the rebellion to come before him. They refuse. *"Is it a small thing that thou hast brought us up out of a land that floweth with milk and honey, to kill us in the wilderness, except thou make thyself a prince over us?"* [96] Their fears for their lives are soon realized. God cleaves the earth, sending the leaders with all their families and possessions down *"into the pit."* As a divine warning to rebels everywhere, the remainder are consumed in fire. The pit and the fire. In the absence of God's miraculous intervention, mass graves in other times and napalm canisters come to mind.

With the fulfillment of Samuel's prophecy, a cry against Saul's kingship does indeed go up. No more than twenty years after Saul's inauguration, a band of the disaffected gathers around David. *"And every one that was in distress, and every one that was in debt, and every one that was discontented, gathered themselves unto him, and he became a captain over them, and there were with him about four hundred men."* [97] The usury of kingship was taking its toll. This time, however, along with history, God would be on the side of the rebels. Saul will be slain and deposed, and the House of David the Judean would succeed that of Saul the Benjaminite. Living under the kingship of one would prove to be little better than under the rule of the other.

Upon the death of Solomon, his son Rehoboam comes to the throne. Not satisfied with the immense wealth accumulated by his father, Rehoboam will go further. *"My father made your yoke heavy,"* he tells people, quite oblivious to the public temper, *"and I will add to your yoke. My father chastised you with whips, but I will chastise you with scorpions."* [98] The consequences were not long in following.

"So Israel rebelled against the house of David unto this day . . . There was none that followed the house of David, but the tribe of Judah only." [99] In 931 b.c., in an unequivocal renunciation of royal elitism, the "congregation" of those who reject Rehoboam and the

House of David, chooses Jeroboam, pointedly the son of a servant in Solomon's palace, to be their king. Comprised of all the tribes that have deserted, the kingdom of Israel is formed to the north of Judah.

In the long run it mattered little. The habiru had fled from corporate society. Whether in Judah or in Israel, they found themselves once again living within it. This time, however, they were bound by custom and heritage to the interests that were seeking to utilize them in the very same fashion as had other corporate houses. Rachmones and all that went with it, so carefully delineated in the laws that Moses introduced, had run smack up against the realities of contractual servitude, and this time there was no escape.

The habiru found themselves in an agonizing situation, with only one real solution available if they were to sustain their collaborative heritage. The same spirit of dissent that had prompted the flight of the habiru from other lands would now be directed at those who sought to dominate them in the place that had become their homeland. Bred of dissent, a spirit of rebellion would plague Israeli rulers throughout the days of the two kingdoms.

In 620 b.c., or thereabouts, the prophet Jeremiah ruefully complains that, *"this people hath a revolting and a rebellious heart. They are revolted and gone."* [100] In classic habiru style, people packed up their political support, and came and went with it as they pleased. Jeremiah's reservations notwithstanding, people had good cause to rebel. Jeremiah himself called down a curse upon those few who exploited the rest. *"Woe unto him that buildeth his house by unrighteousness, and his chambers by wrong, that useth his neighbour's service without wages, and giveth him not for his work."* [101] And so, Jeremiah laments the fate of Jerusalem, *"For the sins of her prophets, and the iniquities of her priests, that have shed the blood of the just in the midst of her."* [102] In the eyes of Jeremiah, the wealthy, prophets and priests alike were all equally culpable. The feelings of very many must have echoed in his protest.

Jeremiah was not alone. Dissent directed against authoritarian practices of the kings prompted a succession of prophets to launch one tirade after another. About 750 b.c. Amos, a herder of Tekoa, attacks those who have *"sold the righteous for silver, and the poor for a pair of shoes . . . and turn aside the way of the meek . . . Woe to them that are at ease in Zion,"* Amos declares, clearly identifying the guilty parties, *" . . . that lie upon beds of ivory and stretch themselves upon their couches, and eat the lambs out of the flock, and the calves out of the midst of the stall."* Expropriating people's sheep and cattle, they turn the profits into providing themselves with luxuries such as only the very wealthy can afford. *"Hear this,"* Amos calls out, *"O ye that swallow up the needy, even to make the poor of the land to fail . . . making the ephah* [bushel] *small, and the shekel great, and falsifying the balances by deceit . . .* [that they] *may buy the poor for silver, and the needy for a pair of shoes."* There is no evidence that Uzziah, king of Judah at the time, or Jeroboam, king of Israel were listening. [103]

Roughly contemporary with Amos, another commoner, Hosea calls the entire community to account. *"Ye have plowed wickedness, ye have reaped iniquity, ye have eaten the fruit of lies, because they didst trust in thy way, in the multitude of thy mighty men."* [104] In these few words, Hosea strikes at the heart of the habiru dilemma. Relying upon the benevolence of the rich and powerful whom they have chosen as rulers, people have fallen victim to their own illusions.

Sometime around 720 b.c., Micah the Morasthite makes it clear that nothing has changed. *"Woe to them that devise iniquity,"* Micah proclaims, *" . . . they covet fields , and take them by violence, and houses, and take them away, so they oppress a man and his house, even a man and his heritage."* All that the habiru have carried with them from one generation to another is threatened. *"Hear, I pray you,"* the prophet beseeches *" . . . ye princes of the house of Israel . . . Who also eat the flesh of my people, and flay their skin from off them, and they break their bones, and chop them in pieces, as for the pot, and as flesh within the caldron."* Micah paints a disturbing picture of the depredation to which the heads of corporate houses have subjected the populace, regrettably no more horrifying than the images with which we are familiar today.

"But in the last days," Micah promises in a passage that so many people since have held close to their hearts, *"... they shall beat their swords into ploughshares, and their spears into pruning hooks. Nation shall not lift up a sword against nation, neither shall they learn war any more. But they shall sit every man under his vine and under his fig tree, and none shall make them afraid."* [105] The paradise that Micah promises is little other than the life that the habiru had enjoyed during the days of the judges. The times had changed, however, and the dream was now capable of being realized only in terms of a collaborative society that functioned on an international scale, heralding indeed the "last days" of corporate rule.

Contemporary with Micah, and reiterating the message of his predecessors, Isaiah, or whoever the prophet may have been whose words were accredited to him, assured his listeners that, *"The Lord will enter into judgment with the ancients of his people, and the princes thereof, for ye have eaten up the vineyard. The spoil of the poor is in your houses. What mean ye that ye beat my people to pieces, and grind the faces of the poor? saith the Lord God of hosts."* At least some of the elders in the community, we may glean from Isaiah, have joined with the princes in "eating up the vineyard." Retribution is on its way, says Isaiah. *"Woe unto them that join house to house, that lay field to field, till there be no place, that they may be placed alone in the midst of the earth."* [106] The inevitable goal of corporate greed, understood even then, was monopolization of all available resources. Retribution would be painfully slow in coming.

Amidst his remarkable visions, about 590 b.c. Ezekiel will take his stand with earlier prophets in excoriating the acts of royalty. First, however, he calls the prophets of his day to account, for *"with lies ye have made the heart of the righteous sad . . . and strengthened the hands of the wicked."* As to the princes of Israel, *"have they dealt by oppression with the stranger . . . vexed the fatherless and the widow . . . taken gifts to shed blood . . . taken usury and increase, and thou hast greedily gained of thy neighbours by extortion . . . Her princes in the midst thereof are like wolves ravening the prey, to shed blood, and to destroy souls, to get dishonest gain."* Ezekiel caps his condemnation of the corporate houses by calling down the customary anathema upon the heads of the perpetrators. *"Woe be to the shepherds of Israel that do feed themselves! Should not the shepherds feed the flocks? . . . but with force and with cruelty you have ruled them."* [107]

From Amos through Ezekiel, we gather that virtually every law which had been introduced by Moses has been transgressed in the rule of the royal houses. Taking the diatribes of the prophets at face value, one might reasonably conclude that the customs of the habiru were pretty much in disarray. If we may judge by the conditions that Nehemiah encountered upon his arrival as governor of Jerusalem from the Persian court at Susa about 430 b.c., such indeed would seem to have been the case.

"And there was a great cry of the people and of their wives against their brethren the Jews," Nehemiah reports. *". . . Some also there were that said, We have mortgaged our lands, vineyards and houses, that we might buy corn, because of the dearth . . . There were also that said, We have borrowed money for the king's tribute, and that upon our lands and vineyards . . . and, lo, we bring into bondage our sons and our daughters to be servants, and some of our daughters are brought unto bondage already, neither is it in our power to redeem them, for other men have our lands and vineyards."* Samuel's prophecy has been more than amply fulfilled. Under Persian rule, the

Jerusalemites are now economically beholden not only to their own corporate houses but to a foreign one as well.

Nehemiah can do nothing to soften Persian oppression. Can he at least persuade the Jewish elite to slacken their hold? *"Then, I consulted with myself, and I rebuked the nobles, and the rulers, and said unto them . . . let us leave off this usury. Restore, I pray you, to them even this day, their lands, their vineyards, and their houses, also the hundredth part of the money, and of the corn, the wine, and the oil, that ye exact of them."* [108] Nehemiah professes to have succeeded.

Like so much else that was unique in habiru and afterwards in Jewish culture, the line of prophets has no parallel anywhere else in the ancient western world. Messiahs would surface here and there to promise the arrival of a new golden age. Oracles, such as the one at Delphi, would issue obscure visions of the future. Nowhere however, save among these contentious people, would prophecy be delivered in plain language, supplying outrage with a historically continuous voice.

Just about the time that the house of David was renounced and the kingdom of the Israelites split in two, we hear the last mention of the 'Apiru in Egyptian texts. In their place we find the culture of the Jews, from then on making its way through corporate society. Within the confines of the world of greed and grab that Bronze-Age empire had initiated, the habiru spirit of dissent was destined to persist. Among others who rejected the major ideological premises of their societies, Einstein, Freud and Marx would live to be its beneficiaries.

Meanwhile, safeguarded within the freedom of mind that dissent made possible, rachmones too survived. In a great, ascending cry, as Samuel predicted and Nehemiah heard, it would echo through the long line of Jewish generations that were to follow, splashing its tears at last against the ruins of a wailing wall. So too, those who stand now and weep before a long, slim wall of black granite in Constitution Gardens. Weeping for the many names inscribed upon it, like the Jews in Jerusalem, they cry as well for lives of loss and suffering everywhere. The sentiment is universal, only waiting to be awakened.

VI Millennium of the Arrival

"They're Asking for CREATIVE CONFORMISTS". So the heading read in 1959 over a lead article in *Nation's Business*. At first glance one might be tempted to qualify this statement as a rampant display of oxymoronic fundamentalism in the realm of corporate culture. Perhaps it is. Creativity relies upon a free spirit and an open mind. Conformity demands an adherence to fixed procedures and a devotion to the rules. How can creativity and conformity share a common milieu?

As it is, for the past four or five thousand years, everywhere in the west, corporate society has served as the dominating milieu. And within its parameters there seems to have been no shortage either of creativity or conformity. The system thrives on infusions of fresh blood into atherosclerotic arteries. Naturally, the relationship between conformity and the creativity functioning within it is quite tenuous.

Employed as a social worker in the San Francisco Department of Social Services, I fancied myself a guerilla within the system. In a way, I was, along with a handful of other disaffected souls, having been instrumental in organizing a voluntary, independent union that provided us all with a shelter for unrestrained whistle-blowing. There was no end to our creativity in revitalizing the old, moribund welfare program. Aiming to pry loose as much as we could in benefits from the system, we made life miserable for an administration that was bent on offering as little as possible to people in need. Many of the activists were Jewish, and in exercising what I now recognize to have been the promptings of rachmones, we made our union into a veritable stronghold of dissent. Bridging the contradiction between creativity and conformity, in campaigning for the things that we felt were right and just, as leverage against the administration we relied principally upon the formal rules and commissioned goals of the agency itself.

Those were the years, 1966 - 1972, when it was fashionable for dissenters to manifest their dissatisfaction with the system by dropping out. As the habiru had done so many centuries before, groups of drop-outs gathered together in collaborative communes, most of them regrettably short-lived. We on the other hand prided ourselves on staying on to fight within the system. The job paid fairly well, and, however forcefully we bent the rules in our favor and those of the welfare recipients, we had only to be careful in not transgressing them as we bent them. Unlikely as the combination may seem, for the short period of our flourishing existence we succeeded quite well in combining rachmones and dissent with benefits and obedience.

Twenty-five years later I obtained a copy of my FBI record. Tucked away within it was a report on our union. Submitted, I feel certain, by an upper level administrator in the Welfare Department, it was surprisingly perceptive of the role that we were playing. "The SSEU talks the language of militant trade-unionism," the informant reported, and "has no professional identification with the agency, contrary to professional social work teaching in schools of social work. The outstanding characteristic of members of this union is that they over-identify with clients and under-identify with the agency. They do not have a professional image of themselves as social workers as distinct from recipients of aid, and this, this reporter feels, is a truly revolutionary step for social workers."

Though hardly endorsing it, the FBI informant accurately grasped the situation. We "over-identified" with our clients, the welfare recipients, while "under-identifying" with the agency. Little as any of us were aware of it at the time, in "over-identifying" with welfare clients, we were extending sentiments of rachmones, much as the habiru had done to the poor, needy and strangers in their midst. At the same time, "under-identifying" with the agency, we were rejecting the outlook of the corporate entity that was responsible for the rules under which we worked. Remaining within the system, we were freeing ourselves from its hold on our thinking. Nor, as the FBI informant noted, did we attach ourselves to organized labor, professional associations or political parties. Within the limits set by our employment in the welfare agency, we were as free as the habiru had been in pursuing the urgings of our hearts. Rachmones on the one hand, dissent on the other. In the estimation of the informant, this was a "truly revolutionary step," one however, I can now understand, in which we breathed new life into a 4000 year old heritage.

"It is this reporter's impression that the aim of the SSEU is truly revolutionary," the informant reiterates later in the report. "It seeks to place the dept. administration on the defensive, prove them wrong on every point possible, attack them openly, remorselessly, and viciously, even slanderously." Echoing through these allegations, substantially correct, one can detect the fulminations of Micah, Hosea, Jeremiah and all the rest of the prophets, launching their tirades against princes and kings.

"Ultimately," the FBI informant concludes, the union aims to "bring about a breakdown of the authority of the administration, and a redistribution of power in the agency into the hands of the most radical element and is something borrowed from the thinking of Marxism, I am certain." The informant errs. Most of us had left Marx far behind, nor had we any illusions of garnering power for ourselves within the agency. We were sufficiently realistic to consider power in running the Welfare Department quite beyond our grasp, and not of a kind that suited us. Our strength was collaborative, endowing us with a type of power that was quite incapable of operating an agency which by its very nature was contractual and corporative.

While our experience in this most maverick of trade unions was exhilarating, in the end we were exhausted. Our "revolutionary" venture slipped quietly away into history. Under the best conditions, one is led to conclude, there are limits as to how successfully rachmones and dissent can thrive within the confines of "benefits and obedience." However heroically dedicated the endeavor, burn-out is virtually assured.

●

Struggling for common human decency in the heart of the welfare system, contending with administration, welfare commissioners and elected officials "on every point possible," it scarcely seemed to me that I was contributing to the well-being of the system. Such was the case however. Within the framework of corporate society there is no way out of this trade-off. Well in advance of tie-less executives and sleeveless computer programmers, we succeeded in abolishing the departmental dress code, doing our bit to prepare the way for the permissiveness that now makes corporate employment more agreeable. I have no doubt that our "revolutionary" efforts assisted the department in adjusting its approach to the demands of the needy. One can only guess at the degree of tension that we diffused between the agency and the community of the poor. As much as administrators hated us for threatening their power, we were doing their work for them. They were in charge of conformity. We had a handle on creativity.

Conformity, in a word, cannot for an instant survive without recruiting creativity. In its turn, creativity cannot flourish in corporate society without a degree of dissent protecting it against the demands of conformity. Everywhere in corporate culture a continuous state of contention therewith prevails between impulses of creativity upon which the vitality of the corporation depends, and the requirements of conformity to which the corporation owes its very existence.

In a perfect world, creativity would require no safeguards other than the exercise of ordinary species alertness in dealing with one's environment. In corporate society, the effective uses of creativity require dissent as a means of keeping conformity at bay. Under these conditions, and they are essentially all we have known since the coming of Bronze-Age empires, the spirit of dissent serves as a medium through which creativity is able to manifest. The more deeply rooted the readiness to dissent, the broader the realm in which creativity can function. Temperaments less beholden to the restrictive premises in which corporate society binds the mind are more comfortable with innovation.

It is in this context that the Jewish celebration of Passover is perhaps best appreciated. Central to an understanding of the Jewish psyche, the passage out of Egypt was something more than merely an escape from slavery. Freeing themselves from the world of Egyptian chariots and archers, the fleeing children of Israel embraced a vision of freedom from rigid mentality and authoritarian bondage. When the waters of the Red Sea closed behind them, trapping their pursuers, the Israelites were locked out forever from a return to the soul-searing complicity of mindless subservience to the institutes of command and control. This heritage, derived from habiru disaffection and firmed up in Mosaic law, has long afforded Jews an opportunity for freeing the mind in the midst of conformity.

Within the workings of corporate society, we ought therefore not be surprised to find a trio such as Marx, Freud and Einstein penetrating the barriers of commonly accepted belief. [110] Nor have we reason to wonder at the likes of Joseph, perfecting the operations of corporate society for Pharaoh. Dissent, it seems, works equally well in defying the rules, as in transforming them for the sake of their preservation. In contemporary terms, one can sight a pair of modern Josephs in two creative personalities making the way smooth for the global spread of American corporate society, Ari Fleischer acting as front man for George W. Bush, while Paul Wolfowitz formulates plans behind the scenes for Dick Cheney.

Whether as Joseph in Egypt or Fleischer and Wolfowitz in America, however freely Jews may offer their services to corporate interests, at a fundamental level their zealously preserved strains of rachmones and dissent compel them to be critical of the corporate systems that most others so readily accept. It is here, I believe, that we may look for the sources of "anti-Semitism" and an answer to the "Jewish question." As with many other seemingly irrational expressions of hatred, "anti-Semitism" emerges in the fury that true-believers direct against those who fail to share their convictions. With its origins in habiru society, one then can readily understand the distaste that so many Westerners harbor for Jews and their culture. In expressions of rachmones Jews are inclined to "over-identify' with the needy. Meanwhile in demonstrations of dissent they are likely to "under-identify" with the corporate structure that enriches itself upon the needy. Worse still, they are "outsiders" and yet, in the creativity of their dissent, they succeed within the very system from which they are disaffected. It is maddening. At one and the same time, as Adolf Hitler often ranted, they are both "communists" and "capitalists." Jews are thus a ready target for the frustration and anger that corporate society massively induces. So long as a culture of habiru values exists side by side with societies of corporate compliance, we can expect the hatred of Jews to persist. [109]

As it is, free or indentured, everyone who works today, works within the conditions that are imposed by corporate society. However noble the evasive tactics that we may devise, one way or another, we are all "working for the man." At the same time, we genuinely believe that our efforts are changing things for the better. Probably they are. People moan over instances of "regression." The horrors of human brutality notwithstanding, however, everything that happens, one may conclude, is progress. Those who by inclination, heritage or tradition feel themselves more at ease in adopting an attitude of dissent, are likely to be more capable of gracing the passage of progress with a measure of benevolence.

·

Reluctant as I am to step into Jewish affairs in the land of Canaan of these days, it would be less than honest of me to say nothing. I am not an Israeli fighting for my life in a hostile environment. I have no desire to tell other people what's best for them to be doing. Nevertheless, professing to explore the sources of the Jewish heritage, I can hardly excuse myself from the responsibility of examining the way in which that heritage might impact upon the decisions being made in Israel by the heirs of the habiru.

"It never dawned on me," playwright Arthur Miller said, "or, I think, on most people, that the new Israel, as a state governed by human beings, would behave more or less the same as any state had acted down through history - defending its existence by all means thought necessary and even expanding its borders when possible." Miller was accepting Jerusalem Prize honors for literary achievement in the field of freedom of the individual in society. Jewish himself, Miller was disappointed in the expansionist path that Israel had taken. With hopes that Israel might yet find its way back to its Jewish roots, he entitled his talk, *"Why Israel must choose justice: without it, no state can endure as a representative of the Jewish nature."* [111]

In its flight from all the many venues of oppression that surrounded the Bronze-Age cradle of its birth, Jewish nature was truly a child of justice. I knew as much from my father. A court stenographer in the New York City municipal justice system, he had a reputation, my mother often took pride in recalling, of unswerving honesty, refusing to add or delete so much as a comma from the testimony that was presented, whether for the sake of defendant or prosecution.

Miller hopes for a climate of justice in the Israeli state. Adhering to justice as a touchstone in their dealings with one another, however, the habiru did so as stateless citizens. Statelessness was their origin and the source of the name by which they were known in the states from which they had fled. No sooner had the habiru established a state of their own, than the justice in which they were conceived fell to the predation of those in whose hands the state was placed. However successful one may be in exercising rachmones, which after all is the heartbeat of Jewish justice, within the confines of a state one is bound at some point to fail.

No more than any other people, not even in the American democracy by which de Tocqueville was so intrigued, can the new Israelites ever succeed in resolving the contradiction between justice and statehood. Not in this world, with whatever good intentions, where boundaries must be defended, investments compounded, and a citizenry kept in check. By the very nature of things as they exist today, the state is compelled to act as a corporate rather than collaborative entity. As surely as justice is "representative of the Jewish nature," injustice is built into the state. In the stateless Time of the Judges there was justice.

Certainly, when Israeli tanks and armored carriers tear through the streets of Gaza, Ramallah and Benin, they rumble also through my heart. Nevertheless, with Arthur Miller, I cannot help but feel deeply for Israel and the Israelis. The death of each and every Israeli, slain in a random killing, is a death inside me. They are my people, and I would like to see their state survive. So long as Jewish voices ring with dissent in the streets and cafes of Tel Aviv, its continued presence in the world will be a contribution to everyone. I also know that the future of our species and this planet does not lie with the survival of Israel or any other state. Whatever may be in store for the state of Israel, something much greater than the state will survive, as it has for so very long a time. In a world without states, history may well account statelessness to have been the paramount and most abiding legacy of the Jews.

Working through the material in this essay, experiencing its surprises and rewards, at some point I realized how profoundly I love my people. When years ago I first became acquainted with the life of the habiru, I felt pride in the roots from which I'd come, and the people of which I was a part. Loving them was something new. My bosom radiant in warmth, the feeling seemed little different from any other of the loves in my life. The heart, after all, is designed to be open, a portal for love to pass in and out, like the angels on Jacob's ladder, going up and down, with intimations of alchemy.

Love for one's people, and pride in their achievements, I believe, heralds the coming of a new state of being for everyone. We live now in the Millennium of the Arrival, not of one people or another, nor of a messiah, though more than a few of them will vie for our attention, but of our species. We are engaged, all of us, in a vast process, wending our way into the next phase in the making of the human species. As the evolution of ourselves takes shape, sooner or later we will all dissolve into it. Ethnic identity, however seemingly distinct or disparate, will lose itself in the fiery cauldron of a new beginning.

Suppressed for thousands of years beneath the sway of corporate imperialism, peoples everywhere today have modern weaponry at their disposal. Equipped with ingeniously devised instruments of modern fire power, they are able to conduct revolts that in the past were almost certain to fail. Supplied with weapons of explosive destructiveness, the horrors in which peoples today mistreat each other in struggling for self-expression, awful as they may be, are likely birth pangs of our arrival as a species. Each people striving to assert itself in the face of others, is doing little else than fashioning itself to this end. Discovering its roots, asserting its ethnicity and identity in the midst of all the rest upon a planet whose society of human beings is fast going global.

The different "races," one might rightfully say in the language of religion, are the Ten Fingers of God, each with its own excellence to contribute and its own shortcomings to temper. The nature of the social fabric that these "races," in their exquisite variety, will learn to weave together is yet to be seen. Fulfillment of the process is a long way off. Certainly, the contractual and conformist arrangements through which corporate society flourishes will need to be dismantled and transformed into peacefully collaborate modes of existence. Liberation of the spirit is on the agenda. Even a millennium is perhaps too short a span of time in which to anticipate the outcome. Meanwhile, looking forward to the eventuality, we each can search out and celebrate our heritage, offering the best of ourselves as a gift to the merger of all.

By virtue of their very origin in statelessness, the Jewish people are uniquely positioned for impacting positively upon the great coherence towards which the species is moving. Einstein, Freud and Marx were all children of the diaspora, honing their intellects on alien beliefs. And us too, we who trace our heritage to the original children of a diaspora, those wild spirits and untamed souls who fled the many lands of sit--and-obey, and banded together in Canaan. The diaspora is a place in our hearts as it was in theirs. We carry it with us wherever we go. Slanders and curses chilling our bones, inquisitions and pogroms, synagogue burnings, laws of exclusion and laws of containment, all have failed to dampen our spirit, holocausts have been unable to still our souls. We are international bankers, yes, in the free trade of ideas, marketing dissent in the service of rachmones. Now as never before both are required. [112]

•

In our own lifetime, the species' search for an identity, savage or sweet, living freely for itself, or indentured to powers and entities beyond itself, now approaches a desperate juncture. Hardest of all, may be the necessity ultimately of discarding ritual and religion. "Imagine," as John Lennon eloquently sang, learning to live without the devotional glue that has both held us together and kept us apart for so long. At last then we may come to appreciate the splendid fullness that is ourselves. [113]

In the final analysis, it seems to me, we are all protoplasm, garbing ourselves in suits of ego, artfully engaged in doing a dance with the world. Passing beyond all the ventures and relationships into which we lead this protoplasm, delving deeply enough, having neither name nor shape, one comes upon a place of utter fullness, an intensity of presence within a lightness of being. One enters a realm of sheer protoplasm, that seeks nothing better than to flourish peacefully, neither in a state of contention nor in one of submission, simply feeling good, and, oh yes, occasionally a bit better than good, experiencing the harmony in life that comes with rightful living.

Aggression, predation and deceit may at times seem satisfying. For myself, after decades of dispute with public officials, administrators and self-appointed gurus, I finally realized that antagonistic confrontation was not healthful. Win or lose, at a cellular level I could feel my juices roiling while my tissues shrank. Like "girls," as songstress Cindi Lauper let everyone know, it seems that protoplasm "just wants to have fun." At the deepest biological level "having fun" appears to mean little other than living peaceably, a condition of course not all that easily arrived at in our societies of combat and control.

Attaining a state of inner peace, free of confrontational engagements, does not necessarily imply diluting the outlook of dissent. On the contrary, responding to oppression and injustice, while maintaining oneself free of myth and delusion, is enhanced in a climate of calm. Adversarial postures at rest, one is able to accept everything into awareness, knowing that one's critical faculty is always on the alert in sorting out the wheat from the chaff. Neither quiescent nor dispassionate, with enthusiasm and joy one surfs the circumstances. Encountering the toxic implacable, in a martial arts of heart and mind, one steps aside.

Through it all, whether in compassion or dissent, passion flows. *"There is no harm in the word compassionate,"* St. Augustine allowed, *"when there is no passion in the case."* [114] In this briefly stated doctrine, one can detect the bounds of compassion beyond which the exercise of rachmones freely passes. Augustine excludes sentiments of passion from expressions of compassion. Rachmones, on the other hand, arises in passion, lives in passion, perishes in its absence. So too dissent. In the quiet of one's heart, the passion of dissent radiates as surely as the passion of rachmones. There is a thrill in stepping beyond the horizon. In either instance, rachmones or dissent, life asserts itself. After 77 years, retired in the aloha clime, I've gone far in mellowing. The harshness now softened in which my soul so long had been gripped, I am still no less an iconoclast and no more a conservative than I was at the age of 17. The edge is off, but the fire burns.

No longer requiring the imprimatur of religious doctrine, or the convoluted reasoning of well-intentioned soothsayers, morality then emerges as a biological imperative. This living flesh thrives in its environment, fails to survive, or languishes in a half-life. One cannot say, This does not matter, That does not matter, hoping to find peace behind the veil of one's indifference. In the interest of "having fun," to protoplasm everything matters. In total submission to the reality of one's being, the heritage of the habiru, the I AM, finally finds a home.

One last story about my grandmother. Not long before her death, she and I were sitting side by side on the living room couch in our Bronx apartment. The occasion was a family reunion, perhaps during Passover in the Spring of 1946. My grandmother's five children were there, my mother and her four brothers, along with their wives and children. Sipping Manichevitz grape wine and heavily scented honey mead, the adults milled about, bickering as usual. A few months previously in an address at Fulton, Missouri, Winston Churchill had turned a phrase, "Iron Curtain," that set the stage for the Cold War. Differences of opinion were being sharply polarized. Voices rising and tempers flaring, the bickering in our living room escalated into acrimony. Looking about and taking all this in, sad of eye and settling close to me, my grandmother quietly said, "For the children I have no more hope, for the grandchildren, maybe." I wonder what she would say today.

Life is a serious business. Enjoy it.

Kapa'au, Hawai'i. 12/12/03

Footnotes

[1] *Genesis* 37.5 - 47.20. Biblical quotations are from the King James version.

[2] "When Something Is Wrong With My Baby". Isaac Hayes and David Porter. 1966. On *Rhythm Country and Blues.* 1994.

[3] Abba Eban. *Heritage: Civilization and the Jews.* 1984.

[4] The peaceable nature of paleolithic hunter-gatherer culture is reviewed in R. Brian Ferguson, "The Birth of War". *Natural History,* July-Aug. 2003. There is strong evidence that the Cro-Magnon hunter-gatherers ordinarily perceived not only the forms of animals, but their energy patterns as well. While this can be surmised, I feel, from their cave paintings and bone carvings, it is plainly visible in the rendering of the shaman from the cave of *Trois Freres,* about 12,000 b.c. Copied by Henri Breuil, the figure contains brush strokes that are virtually identical with the streaming ch'i currents of the microcosmic and macrocosmic orbits pictured in Chinese texts. A continuity of this awareness is indicated around 3000 b.c in the Iceman of Ötztal Alps. Tatoo marks along the backbone and ankles of this unfortunate mountaineer correspond to acupuncture points that lie along the ch'i meridians. Similar tatoo marks were discovered on the body of a Scythian chieftain, buried at Pazyryk in southern Siberia about 400 b.c. Chinese medicine and martial arts both had their origin in shamanic lore, suggesting at least a partial heritage in the perception of energy currents from paleolithic times to our own. The faculty of perceiving the flow of living energy, which nowadays is practiced by some body workers and healers would then, however, have prevailed as a cultural trait. One wonders what sort of society might have displayed so vital a faculty in its members. Among modern practitioners similar skills accompany extreme openness and sensitivity, qualities that one would hardly think likely to have been widespread in a predatory or repressive culture. This is not to suppose that our paleolithic ancestors were "noble savages," or possessed of any other scarcely attainable human virtue. They must have been pretty much like us, for they were us, without however going to war with each other. In these times, if one cares to try it as a thought experiment, one can imagine how life might have been led and psyches formed in the absence of warfare spanning a stretch of 20,00 years.

[5] Hunter-gatherer culture owed its unity over vast distances to a commonly pursued mode of sustenance in a relatively uniform habitat. It thrived on a shared ecology. The glacial melt that initiated the mesolithic era resulted in a variety of

specific habitats that made for different ecological niches. Seashore, lakes, plains, forests, mountain slopes, each with its own particular flora and fauna, offered specific biospheres to would-be settlers. Local cultures evolved as adaptations to the requirements of survival in each place. A similar process is familiar to biologists in instances of local adaptation, members of a species isolated within a specific habitat evolving in response to the opportunities for survival that are available in their environment. The evolution of "Darwin's finch" from a single species into thirteen on the Galapagos is historically the type case. From another point of view, Karl Marx maintained as a general rule that the nature of human consciousness is conditioned by people's relation to the means of production. Agrarian economy, Marx suggested, evoked one system of values and beliefs, the industrial economy quite another. Contrasts in consciousness likewise would be expected between slaves and masters, as also between managers, workers producing hard goods, and those employed in software. The varieties of taste that differentiate "high brow," "low brow" and "middle brow" are assiduously researched by marketing agencies. When I grew up in New York City, during the 40s and 50s, word on the street had it that rich folks were Yankee fans, blue collar workers rooted for the Giants, while, win or lose, service-employed minorities, day laborers and disaffected intellectuals stuck with the Dodgers. Class warfare touched base all around the ballpark diamond. Pursuing a livelihood in specific situations, human beings have been known to adapt as inventively as did Darwin's finch or any other species. For an excellent discussion of mesolithic culture, see *World Atlas of Archaeology*, 1985, James Hughes, Exec. Ed. "The First Bowmen of the European Forests".

[6] See Ryan, William B.F. And Pitman , Walter C. *Noah's Flood: The New Scientific Discoveries about the Event that Changed History.* 1998. In 1925 the reality of the Great Flood became an issue in the famous Monkey Trial that the State of Tennessee conducted against school master John Scopes. Accused of teaching Charles Darwin's theory of evolution, Scopes was defended by internationally famous criminal lawyer Clarence Darrow. The state was represented by the celebrated orator William Jennings Bryan. Here is a short excerpt from the court proceedings as I recall it. It's the single exchange in the trial that stuck in my mind. Darrow is directing a question to Bryan.

> DARROW: *According to the Bible, except for those taken aboard the Ark by Noah, all living creatures drowned. Do you believe that, sir?*
> BRYAN: *Yes, I do.*
> DARROW: *Including the fishes, Mr. Bryan?*
> BRYAN: [Pause] *Yes, sir, the fishes too.*

Laughter shakes the courtroom, and reading an account of the trial I laughed too. How absurd the grand orator, congressman, secretary of state and candidate for president had been. How cleverly incisive the great lawyer. Religious fundamentalism had suffered a blow, I felt, from which it could not possibly recover. And yet, it now appears, the biblical account is essentially correct. Not only did all terrestrial creatures drown that had been unable to reach higher ground when the Gates of the Bosporus gave way, but so indeed did the fish. Especially the fish. They could not survive in the salt water that poured into their sweet water habitat. Bryan died shortly after the trial. Darrow never again showed up in court. Lessons abound against pride, hubris and just plain ordinary smugness. Listen to everyone, laugh at no-one, form your own conclusions.

[7] For an overview of the early farming communities see Gimbutas, Marija. *The Language of the Goddess*. 1998. Introduction. Also, Foreword by Joseph Campbell.

8] Jean Bottero. *Archives Royale de Mari*. 1955. My translation.

[9] Isaac Mendelsohn. *Bull. Amer. Soc. Orient. Res*. 143.

[10] Donald J. Wiseman. *The Alalakh Tablets*. 1953.

[11] M. Lejeune. "Les Forgerons de Pylos." *Historia*. X. My translation.

[12] D.L. Page. *History and the Homeric Iliad*. 1959.

[13] A. Goetze. "Warfare in Asia Minor." *Iraq*. XXV.

[14] Isaac Mendelsohn. *Slavery in the Ancient Near East*. 1949.

[15] Nelson Glueck. *The Other Side of the Jordan*. 1940.

[16] It might be objected that the economic systems operated and controlled by Bronze-Age dynasts are not "real corporations." After all, they offered no shares on the market, there were no stockholders or board of directors, and so on. Elaborated around the root *corp*, the word would imply a body, group or aggregate of persons acting together. As defined in *Merriam-Webster's*, rev.2002 , a **corporation** is 1. *"a body of persons associated for some purpose"* . . . 2a. Roman and Civil Law: *"a group of persons or objects treated by law as an individual or unity having rights or liabilities distinct from those of the persons or objects composing it"* . . . 3. US. Common and status law: *"a body formed and authorized by law to act as a single person and endowed by law with the capacity of succession,"* also known as a **"corporation aggregate."** . . . *On the other hand, a corporation may be* 2b. *"a single person or object treated by the law as having a legal individuality or entity other than that of a natural person."* In this case it may be defined as a **"corporation sole"**: *"a corporation consisting of only*

one person." To this, *hyperdictionary. com* adds: *"A corporation sole consists of a single person, who is made a body corporate and politic, in order to give him some legal capacities, and especially that of succession, which as a natural person he cannot have. Kings, bishops, deans, parsons and vicars, are in England sole corporations."* Corporations may thus be formed when an aggregate body is legally accorded the status of a person, or where a person is politically constituted as a body. In according the monarch divine status, distinct from any private obligations to which he might otherwise be subject, the Mesopotamian *Epic of Creation*, as we will see, does just this. As is the case with a contemporary industrial or financial corporation, the Bronze-Age dynast procured raw materials, had them manufactured into useable products and assigned their distribution. It's important to recognize the continuity of corporate control and corporate culture from the Bronze Age onward, as signaling a major departure from prior society and remaining so until our own times. It would follow then that all literature, philosophy and religion from that era to our own can fully be understood only in the context of this continuity, whether in compliance or as dissent.

[17] Ashurnasirpal II. *Annals*. About 875 b.c.

[18] The scene is reproduced in James B. Pritchard, Editor. *The Ancient Near East, Volume 1, An Anthology of Texts and Pictures*. 1958.

[19] E.I. Gordon. *Sumerian Proverbs: glimpses of everyday life in ancient Mesopotamia*. 1959.

[20] The value of communal harmony has been built into the human brain. As revealed in MRI explorations on people during cooperative game playing, a rupture in social inclusion registers quite literally as an experience of physical injury. When a person is excluded from the game, an augmented flow of blood occurs to the anterior cingulate cortex of the brain, indicating increased activity in that area. This is accompanied by feelings of distress, and the greater the feeling of distress that's reported, the more profoundly this section of the brain has been activated. The same area of the brain activates during the "aversive experience of physical pain." Neurologically, then, the consequences of social exclusion can be as painful as bodily injury. Accompanied by "separation distress cries," similar neural reactions are observed in dogs, guinea pigs, chicks, rats and primates other than human. Biological sources of collaborative behavior thus have an ancient history among mammals. Continuously elaborated during past millions of years, the neural response to social rejection and the loss of collaborative harmony is likely to be all the more emotionally distressful in humans. In our cultures of alienation and dysfunction, where instances of rejection and exclusion are pervasive, socially inspired cerebral pain must be a common occurrence. Occupying a prominent place in the psychopathology of everyday life, in dealing with that pain one can

expect the entire assemblage of ego defenses to be marshaled. See Naomi I. Eisenberger, Matthew D. Lieberman and Kipling D. Wilson, "Does Rejection Hurt? An fMRI Study of Social Exclusion," *Science*, #302, 10/10/03.

[21] Thorkild Jacobsen. *The Treasures of Darkness: A History of Mesopotamian Religion.* 1976. Translations cited from the text of the *Enuma elish* are primarily his.

[22] Susan Preston Blier. "The Place Where Vodun Was Born". *Natural History,* 10/95.

[23] When the divine monarch of ancient Mesopotamia sliced open the still fecund carcass of the Mother of Waters, he did more than merely detach the things of heaven from those of earth. In severing the dismembered halves of Tiamat, the warrior-king also created a gap in human awareness that would go down through time as a separation of body and mind. In the world of collaborative society, body and mind had served together in a functional unity of the entire human being. No separation existed then between thought and action. As people went about their daily tasks, made plans, worked or played together, all happened as one in response to circumstances and need. "*At that time,*" Chinese taoist Huai Nan Tzu wrote about 125 b.c. regarding a similar state of affairs that had prevailed in his own land, "*there was no special governing authority to give decisions, the people lived their lives in quiet retirement, and things came to fruition of themselves. The world was an undifferentiated unity, the pure collectivity had not been broken up and dispersed, the different sorts of people formed a oneness, and all creation flourished exceedingly.*" People experienced the flow of life as an uninterrupted process of transformation and change.

With the splitting of Tiamat, this organically unified mode of existence would no longer be the case. The organic integrity of collaborative society had been shattered. In its stead, bodies of the populace could be assigned to specific labors, while legal strictures, social imperatives and mythic constructs were designed to occupy their minds. At his own pleasure, the divinely invested ruler might freely manipulate both.

In the course of time, as people thought about these things, "nature" and "nurture" were regarded as disparate factors in the process of being and becoming,   the "spiritual" and "material"were parceled out into mutually exclusive realms, while "energy" and "mass" were treated as alternative realities and light was regarded as sometimes a "particle" and on other occasions a "wave." One of these twin pairs was present, or the other, never both together as complementary aspects of a unitary phenomenon. Classically formulated in the West by Aristotle, a mandate of either/or was predicated in logic and science. The "excluded middle," the grey area in which all the action occurred, was banished from consideration,. Each of these fractures of awareness, and others as well, followed upon the separation of body and mind. Discomfited by the unworkability of their detachment one from the other, philosophers and scientists thenceforth set about the task of discovering a way to rejoin them. For its part, whether cosmic or angelic, religion would resurrect their unity in the hereafter. Subject to the mindset of corporate culture to which the separation of body and mind adheres, in this world all such efforts have been doomed to fail. No more readily than the scattered shards of Humpty and Dumpty, can they simply be put back together again.

It's perhaps as a measure of solace for our lack of success in reuniting the sundered halves of body and mind, that we sigh with relief when the beautiful lady emerges once again whole from the magician's box. As it is, only in a restoration of collaborative existence, such as existed prior to the Tiamatic Split, is a unity of awareness likely to reemerge, quite naturally then "of itself."

[24] In a work first published in German in 1887, *Gemeinschaft und Gesellschaft*, and translated into English as *Community and Association,* Ferdinand Tönnies examined the contrast between collaborative and corporate society. "The relationships which come to us in nature," Tönnies wrote describing Gemeinschaft, "are in their essence mutual, are fulfilled in mutual performance . . . Gemeinschaft as a bond of 'blood' is in the first place a physical relation." On the other hand, "In the conception of Gesellschaft the original or natural relations of human beings to each other must be excluded." Relationships are primarily contractual, with each one "thinking of himself and trying to bring to the fore his importance and advantages in competition with the others. . . Gemeinschaft should be considered as a living organism," Tönnies asserts, "Gesellschaft as a mechanical aggregate and artifact." The absolutism of the Bronze-Age corporate state is faithfully perpetuated in the consequences. "The entire culture has been transformed into a civilization of state and Gesellschaft, and, " Tönnies warns, "this transformation means the doom of culture itself if none of its scattered seeds remain alive and again bring forth the essence and idea of Gemeinschaft, thus secretly fostering a new culture amidst the decaying one." Recognizing their compromised nature in corporate society, Tönnies nonetheless sees the scattered seeds of Gemeinschaft preserved in trade unions and cooperatives, much as they were during Greco-Roman times. For their part, corporations often seek to project evidences of Gemeinschaft. "Team work" is ever the buzz word of the day. Nowhere perhaps has the irony of this attempt been more blatantly exhibited than in the case of I.G. Farben, in full: *Interessen Gemeinschaft Farbenindustrie Aktiengesellschaft -* Community of Dye Industries, Incorporated. "Professor Erwin Selck, a member of the supervisory board of directors [and leader of a company of SS cavalry] tried to explain it to American investigators," who were interviewing him after the defeat of Nazi Germany. "'Community of interest: working together for the common good, cooperation. You understand?' he said, and his grim, death's head face cracked into a smile." In Richard Sasuly, *IG Farben*, 1947.

[25] In Samuel N. Kramer. "The Biblical *Song of Songs* and the Sumerian love songs". *Expedition,* 5.

[26] In Jacobsen.

[27] In James B. Pritchard, *Ancient Near Eastern Texts Relating to the Old Testament,* 1955.

[28] These and the quotations from texts regarding the SA.GAZ/habiru that follow are taken from James B. Pritchard, *Ancient Near Eastern Texts Relating to the Old Testament,* 1955; J.B. Pritchard, editor, *The Ancient Near East. Volume 1: An Anthology of Texts and Pictures,* 1958; William L. Moran, *The Amarna Letters,* 1987; William F. Albright. "From Patriarch to Moses, Part I: From Abraham to Joseph." *Bibl. Arch.,* 1973, and others as cited. The *Jewish Virtual Library* has a brief discussion of habiru/Hebrew relations, "Who Were the Hebrews?" by Gerald A. Larne along with a bibliography. www.us-israel.org/jsource/History /hebrews.html.

[29] For a remarkable review of popular disaffection with corporate rule in Greek, Roman and Biblical times see C. Osborne Ward, *The Ancient Lowly,* 1907, Charles H. Kerr, publisher. Ward also presents a meticulously detailed account of the alternative life styles common to ancient trade unions and fraternal societies organized by the tens of thousands, in which the free, the slave and the poor counted equally. In their practices of egality and sharing, elements of the collaborative character of hunter-gathering and early farming cultures are readily discernible. For further documentation of the immense number of guilds and trade unions in Near Eastern and Greco-Roman antiquity see especially Jean Pierre Waltzing, *Étude historique sur les corporations professionelles chez les Romains."* Published in 1896, this monumental work has never been translated, a telling commentary on academic tunnel vision. Also see M.N. Tod, *Sidelights on Greek History,* 1937; R. Meiggs, *Roman Ostia,* 1971; C. Virolleaud, *Le Palais Royal d'Ugarit: Textes en Cuneiformes Alphabatiques,* 1965; A.E.R.Boak, "Gilds in Greco-Roman Egypt", *Trans. Amer. Philol. Assoc.,* LXV; Isaac Mendelsohn, "Gilds in Babylonian and Assyria", *Jnl. Amer. Or. Soc.,* 60. In Asia Minor, home of the Hittites, W.M. Ramsay notes in *Asianic Elements in Greek Civilization,* 1927, "unions are older than cities, and lasted longer." The entire subject of trade unions in antiquity, occupying in people's lives as they did, a major alternative to the corporate society in which they were embedded, has been allowed to languish in dated texts.

[30] William F. Albright, translation. In Pritchard, 1958.

[31] *Leviticus.* 19.18.

[32] *Genesis.* 12.16, 14.13.

[33] *Ezekiel.* 16.3, reiterated in 16.45.

[34] *I Chronicles.* 16.19-20.

[35] J. Bottero. *Le Probleme des Habiru a la 4e Rencontre Assyriologique Internationale.* 1954. My translation.

[36] *I Samuel.* 9.12-13. In addition to sacrificial meals in "high places," a striking testimony to habiru communal practice has been preserved in Ethiopia. There among the Ethiopian Christians, Jewish Falasha and "Hebraeo-Pagan" Qemant, all thought to have been inspired by ancient migrants from Canaan, we catch glimpses of what life may have been like among the pre-monarchical habiru. Around 470 b.c., based upon a Canaanite influx into this region that evidently began many centuries earlier, a Jewish kingdom was established in northern Ethiopia. Along about 330 a.d. much of the populace converted to Christianity, nevertheless continuing to this day with practices, such as the interdiction of labor on the sabbath, that are essentially Judaic. Appearing unmistakably to predate the Israelite monarchy, they suggest a habiru origin.

Much of the history of the Ethiopian Jews and their Christianized fraction is detailed by Graham Hancock in *The Sign and the Seal*, 1992. Most compellingly of interest is Hancock's account of the *Timkat* festival that is celebrated annually in Christian communities. On this day a *tabot*, symbolically replicating the Ark of the Covenant, is brought forth from each temple and publicly displayed. On January 18, 1990 Hancock witnessed the celebration of *Timkat* in the Ethiopian city of Gondar. "Men and women, small children, the very elderly, lame people, obviously sick and dying people, laughing, happy, healthy people - half of Ethiopia seemed to be here," Hancock writes. "Many clutched musical instruments of one kind or another: cymbals and trumpets, flutes and fiddles, lyres and biblical harps." When at length priests emerged bearing the *tabot* from the temples, "the crowd erupted into a frenzy of shouts and stamping feet and, from the women, shrill ululations - a rousing, tremulous vibration . . . Sometimes funnelled through narrow alleyways, sometimes spreading out across patches of open land, sometimes stopping inexplicably, sometimes fast, sometimes slow, always bursting with music and song, we progressed through the ancient city . . . In the space ahead of the *tabot* several impromptu troupes of dancers had formed themselves - some of mixed sex, some all male, some all female, some dressed in everyday working clothes, some in church vestments. At the centre of each of these groups was a drummer, his *kebero* slung around his neck, beating out an ancient and savage rhythm, whirling, jumping, turning and shouting while those around him exploded with energy, leaping and gyrating, clapping their hands, beating tambourines and cymbals, pouring with sweat as they capered and reeled."

Hancock is struck by how faithfully the scene in Gondar recapitulates the description of the occasion when King David and the Israelites installed the Ark of the Covenant in the precincts of Jerusalem. *"And David and all the house of Israel played before the* [ark of the] *Lord on all manner of instruments made of fir wood, even on harps and on psalteries, and on timbrels, and on cornets, and on cymbals."* Avowedly pre-Solomonic, the celebration is almost certainly a vestige of habiru practice, with David himself playing a notable part. *"And David danced before the Lord with all his might . . . So David and all the house of Israel brought up the ark of the Lord with shouting, and with the sound of the trumpet . . . David leaping and dancing before the Lord."* The sight of David cavorting in the streets is more than his wife Michal can bear, *"and she despised him in her heart . . . In the eyes of the handmaids of his servants,"* she declares, David *"shamelessly uncovereth himself."* Michal thenceforth bans the king from her bed. For his part, David assures her that *"of the maidservants which thou hast spoken of, of them shall I be had in honour."* II Samuel. 6.5-22. Defying the establishmentarian outlook of his aristocratic wife, David has cast in his lot with the ordinary folk of the land.

Three thousand years later Hancock sees David's dance about the ark echoed at the *Timkat* festival in Gondar. "Now, urged on by trumpet blasts and by shouts, by the thrum of a ten-stringed *begegna* and the haunting tones of a shepherd's flute, a young man dressed in traditional robes of white cotton performed a wild solo dance . . . Beautiful in his lithe vigour, splendid in his ferocious energy, the youth seemed entranced. With all eyes upon him he circled the pulsing *kebero*, pirouetting and swaying, shoulders jerking, head bobbing, lost in his own inner rhythms, praising God with every limb, with every ounce of his strength, with every particle of his being."

Singing and dancing, playing musical instruments, ecstasy and community, all in all this freely spirited expression of one's religious fervor may well be taken as a remnant survival of habiru society. Habiru culture giving way to dynastic imperatives, no king after David, or for that matter anyone else in the kingdom, would be reported cavorting with such joyous abandon before the Holy of Holies. Religious adoration passed into the confines of the Temple that Solomon built to house the ark. A priesthood would officiate. About the land, people still held communal celebrations in "high places," wary now of assaults launched by armed defenders of a centralized faith that catered to the needs of the powerful.

[37] Bottero. 1954.

[38] *Exodus.* 4.10-12. All quotations in italics are taken unaltered directly from the King James version. Utilizing these passages along with other material in the bible, I've endeavored to reconstruct the emergence of Hebraic cultural identity. In keeping with the account that's delivered in the book of *Exodus*, it's clearly evident that the impact of Moses on this process was instrumental. In arriving at a

reasonable understanding of how the values and practices of a heterogeneous community of rebels and bandits might have evolved into a major cultural identity, I've relied upon two assumptions. Forsaking any efforts rationally to explain the absurd, I've chosen to ignore all biblical references to the miraculous. There is no reason to regard as anything but mythic inventions events such as that of an infant set afloat in an ark of bulrushes and providentially plucked from the Nile by a royal princess, or the succession of plagues that are magically brought about by the shape-shifting rods of Moses and Aaron, frogs, lice, flies, "murrain," boils, hail, locusts, darkness and finally the death of all Egyptian firstborn, much less the marvelous parting of the waters of the Red Sea down to dry ground, and a good deal else that appears in the bible whenever priestly scribes wished to exalt the greatness and power of the Lord, and of course their own indispensability. Biblical scholars and assorted other academicians have devoted much precious time in their attempts to provide natural explanations for these miraculously engendered happenings. Their efforts have come to naught. Disregarding the miraculous, I've matched the passages in the biblical account that seem most congruent with ancient tests such as those from Tell el Amarna, developing, best as I could, a coherent account of the remarkable accomplishments of a society of dissenters.

Secondly, I assume that central among the achievements of these disaffected runaways, and evidently vitally instrumental, was the contribution of Moses. Assigning his impact upon events to the agency of God, demeans the man to exalt the unknown. In the hands of priestly scribes, Moses serves simply as a vehicle of the Lord. Lost in the exchange are his courage, insight and the magnitude of his personal vision. Portraying Moses as an instrument of the Lord, monumentally statured and readily extrapolated by Hollywood extravaganza into the imagery of Charlton Heston, deletes the heroism of an extraordinary human being from its rightful place in history. A thousand years later, in times vastly enriched by literature and the arts, Jesus of Nazareth would benefit by a more straightforwardly reportorial press, even though in his case as well one must read both between and beyond the lines to find another visionary who simply wished to restore the laws of the habiru.

Credit should be given where credit is due, and one must acknowledge that the mythic history spun by the priestly scribes of Israel and Judah was no less a work of genius than the Epic of Creation that had been composed by the priestly scribes of Sumeria. Dramatically divergent from the Epic of Creation, however, embedded in the myth and ritual of the biblical tale, one finds a treasury of folk memories and common human values that could not easily be denied. The legacy of the habiru lived on, and when everything else failed the cry for rachmones would be taken up by a steady stream of furiously dissenting prophets.

[39] *Exodus.* 2.7-10.

[40] *Exodus.* 2.11-15. This and the preceding passages.

[41] *Exodus.* 18.18-22.

[42] *Exodus.* 2.16-22.

[43] Civilization has been afflicted with strangeness. Strangeness inhabits its sinews, plants its sign upon all its undertakings, tempers personal resolve even as it fuels desire. Establishing its presence under conditions of estrangement, strangeness aggrieves the soul with seizures of angst, inexplicably and unreasonably erupts in bursts of anxiety that seem forever lurking, never far beneath the measured calm of adopted facades. Peering into the future, anguish clouds one's vision. Finally, in angina, strangeness exerts itself as a clutch upon the pectoral muscles, driving a failing heart to its terminal contraction.

These words one and all, strangeness/estrangement/angst/anxiety/anguish/angina, are verbal brothers and sisters, cousins sharing space with many other words in the same family that derive from a single root, *ang,* which provides them with their central phoneme. In its deepest sense signifying a strangulation of the spirit, they reveal, in its various aspects, the consequences that follow upon having distanced ourselves from the collaborative relationships with which we were endowed in our species awakening.

Yes, we suffer too in our estrangement from the life of the land, and from the comings and goings of other creatures and living things. All this weighs heavily upon us in the emergence of a phenomenon that we've come more familiarly to speak of as alienation. None counts quite so heavily, however, as the estrangement that we experience from one another in committing ourselves to the contractual arrangements of corporate society. Among all the oddities of our existence, little affects us so profoundly as this strangeness, self-imposed upon the harmony of natural collaboration that we might otherwise be enjoying. So threatened are we by the prospects of unreserved attachment to others and to the life around us, that we devise philosophies of detachment hopefully to dismiss the reality of our psychic impoverishment.

In *The Economic and Philosophical Manuscripts* of 1832, Karl Marx initiated the discussion of alienation from the point of view of the estranged labor that paramountly characterizes corporate, i.e. "class," society. "*Estranged labor,*" Marx wrote, "*not only estranges nature from man and estranges man from himself, from his own function, from his vital activities,* [but] *because of this, it also estranges man from his species . . . from his own body, from nature as it exists outside him, from his spiritual essence, his human existence . . . man from man.*" Translation by Martin Milligan, 1959.

The domain of estrangement described by Marx was of course the "strange land" that the hero of Robert Heinlein's novel encountered. Corporate society was no more amenable to the beleaguered grokker in our own day than it had been to the ancestors of the Hebrews in theirs. With no possibility of escape other than flight, the habiru chose "strangeness in a strange land" over the certainties of far greater estrangement in the societies that surrounded them. In fleeing, they enshrined in their lives something of the collaborative ethos that had passed down to them from more ancient days, evolving it into a cultural preserve against strangulation of the spirit.

In *Destiny and Motivation in Language,* 1954, A.A. Roback explores the occurrence, context and expressive intent of *ng, nk* and other phonemes. For a general review of physiognomics, as a study in the temperamental and somatic sources of behavior and language, see Heinz Werner, *Comparative Psychology of Mental Development.* 1940.

[44] *Exodus.* 3.2-4.

[45] *Exodus.* 3.9-10.

[46] *Numbers.* 12.3.

[47] *Exodus.* 3.13-14.

[48] *The Admonitions of Ipuwer,* excerpts. Papyrus Leiden 334, primary translation by John A. Wilson.

[49] *Exodus.* 5.19 -25.

[50] *Exodus.* 3.9-10. With great regret I've omitted the likely date of Moses' speech or of the Exodus that followed. I've always felt that providing dates for material to which reference is made is indispensable to the reader in meaningfully placing events in their historical context. In the case of the Exodus unfortunately there is now well-grounded reasoning and evidence separating the actual date from that traditionally accepted by no less than 300 years, around 1550 b.c., during the Middle Bronze Age, rather than 1250, in Late Bronze. Under these circumstances it would be a disservice to the reader to offer dates that are only conjecturally correct by a wide margin. A similar concern applies to the letters recovered from Tell el Amarna. Should the earlier date prove to be correct, one would need to locate the reign of Akhenaton considerably later than that of the Exodus. Interestingly enough, this dating would suggest an influence of Mosaic religion upon the solar religion of the sun king, rather than the reverse as is customarily supposed. Instead of Moses acquiring a taste for monotheistic worship in the court of the pharaoh, Akhenaton would have seized upon the attractiveness of habiru religion as an inspiration for his own, converted of course into royal parameters. I must say, this seems to me the more probable train of events. Whether the earlier or later date of the Exodus is taken as correct does not, in my

opinion, substantially affect the historical dynamic through which habiru society passed into Hebraic culture, nor does it impair the significance of Moses in bringing about that transition..

[51] *Exodus*. 6.7.

[52] *Exodus*. 19.5 and *Leviticus*. 26.12

[53] *Psalms*. 86.15.

[54] *Leviticus*. 19.18.

[55] *Leviticus*. 19.13.

[56] *Leviticus*. 25.35-36.

[57] *Leviticus*. 19.35-36.

[58] *Exodus*. 30.15.

[59] *Exodus*. 23.6.

[60] *Leviticus*. 19.15.

[61] *Deuteronomy*. 1.16-17.

[62] *Numbers*. 15.16 and *Leviticus*. 24.22.

[63] *Exodus*. 23.1.

[64] *Numbers*. 35.30.

[65] *Deuteronomy*. 17.6-7.

[66] *Numbers*. 35.6-28.

[67] *Deuteronomy*. 24. 14-15.

[68] *Exodus*. 20.10.

[69] *Exodus*. 21.26-27.

[70] *Leviticus*. 25.9.

[71] *Deuteronomy.* 15.11-14.

[72] *Exodus.* 21.16.

[73] *Deuteronomy.* 23.15-16.

[74] *Deuteronomy.* 24.19-22.

[75] *Leviticus.* 19.9-10.

[76] *Deuteronomy.* 20.19.

[77] *Exodus.* 22.21.

[78] *Exodus.* 23.9.

[79] *Leviticus.* 19.33-34.

[80] *Deuteronomy.* 21.10-14.

[81] *Exodus.* 20.3-5,7.

[82] *Exodus.* 4.12,15.

[83] Dispensing welfare benefits and serving as a social venue, the Workmen's Circle functions very much in the tradition of ancient trade unions, guilds, religious groups and social associations. So too, for that matter, do Wisconsin dairy farm cooperatives, hippie communes and Israeli kibbutzim. History is replete with instances of collaborative society. The proliferation of fraternal organizations astonished de Tocqueville when he visited America in 1831. At least marginally, groups such as Elks, Moose, Kiwanis and Shriners, barnraisings and sewing circles, Greek letter fraternities and gangs in the 'hood, all attest to the vigor of collaborative engagement. Brief as they may be, so too do the non-violent protest groups that function through consensus. Even under the most adverse conditions, the impulses towards this form of society seem never to have been expunged from the human genome. Among all such groups, it seems to me that the Workmen's Circle enjoys a special distinction. Joining the rachmones of social welfare to dissent of the dissatisfied, it prides itself on supporting the "emancipation of workers from oppression and exploitation."

[84] Looking back over the years, I'm coming to appreciate the degree to which my grandmother enjoyed poking fun at the pretensions of her own people.

She often told the tale of a well-to-do Jewish traveler on a railway train in Czarist Russia. This was a time when Jews were largely prohibited from riding on trains. One needed to be somebody special. And so the traveler was quite surprised when the passenger in the seat opposite him, both by appearance and mannerisms, seemed also to be Jewish. Who was this man? Where was he going? Pursuing a convoluted trail of deductive logic that wound its tortuous way through an almost endless series of assumptions and conclusions, each of which my grandmother took great pleasure in reciting one after the other, the Jewish traveler was finally satisfied that he had established the identity of the passenger riding across from him. Now he felt prepared to address this man. "A pleasant good morning to you," he brightly began, "and what business is bringing you to Kiev, Dr. Rudinsky?" Startled, the man wants to know how come the Jewish traveler had known his name, profession and destination. "*Nu?*" So? the self-satisfied traveler smugly responds: "It stands to reason." My grandmother concluded the tale in a gale of laughter. While the story ridicules the excesses of Jewish intellection, it also reveals the extent of its emphasis in Jewish life. I heard it also from another adult in the family.

[85] My grandmother's jocularity was no doubt boosted by the fact that her married name was Kameny, given to her by a husband she considered to be less than ideal. In Slavic, *ka.men.nyi*, the root sound for stone is evidently the central phoneme, *men*. The same phoneme surfaces in *menhir*, the upright stones of Celtic graves and ceremonies, and in *dolmen* - "table-stone," that was laid horizontally across the menhirs. In Egyptian, *men* is likewise stone, and *meni* is a stony hill or mountain. Contemplating employing kameni as a pen name in Hawaii, I discovered that Hawaiian *kameni* actually exists and, transliterated from the English, means cement. The origin of the word is no more readily apparent than is the source of habiru. The connective link in both instances, as in many others whose use spans continents and crosses oceans, ultimately may well be traced to the inner workings of the human body and mind, much the same everywhere around the globe.

[86] I've rendered the English spellings of Yiddish words generally as they are given in Yiddish dictionaries, and in part as I heard them from my grandmother. At any rate, Yiddish has always been so fluid, subject to influences from the many places where Jews have made their home, that linguistic correctness in all instances will likely always remain an elusive goal. From habiru times to our own, flexibility in adaptation has ever served as a basis for preserving an essential culture.

[87] *Proverbs*. 14.13.

[88] *Judges*. 21.25.

[89] *II Kings*. 17.9-10.

[90] *I Samuel*. 8. 4-5, 20.

[91] *I Samuel*. 8.11-17.

[92] *I Samuel*. 8.18-19.

[93] *I Samuel*. 10.24.

[94] *I Samuel*. 11.12.

[95] *Numbers*. 16.2-3.

[96] *Numbers*. 16.13.

[97] *I Samuel*. 22.2.

[98] *I Kings*. 12.14.

[99] *I Kings*. 12.19-20.

[100] *Jeremiah*. 5.23.

[101] *Jeremiah*. 22.13.

[102] *Lamentations*. 4.13.

[103] *Amos*. 2.6-7, 6.1-4, 8.4-6.

[104] *Hosea*. 10.13.

[105] *Micah*. 2.1-2, 3.1-3, 4.3-4.

[106] *Isaiah*. 3.14-15, 5.8.

[107] *Ezekiel*. 13.22, 22.7-12, 34.2-4.

[108] *Nehemiah*. 5.3-5, 7-11.

[109] See Wilhelm Reich, *The Mass Psychology of Fascism*, first published in German in 1933, for his insight into the origins of scapegoating in the authoritarian state and family. In 1956, agents of the FDA, acting under orders to suppress Reich's theories of orgone energy, burned copies of the book along with his other writings.

It is at heart their reluctance to embrace accepted authority, I believe, that has made the Jews everybody's favorite scapegoat. Perhaps more than anything else, it is their respective attitudes towards authority that drives the contrast between Christians and Jews

Authority emerges as a central theme in the Gospels. "*For he taught them as one having authority, and not as the scribes,*" [*Matthew.* 7.29] it is said of Jesus. Jesus himself makes it clear that the authority to which he is appealing is that of "*Moses and the prophets.*" [*Luke.* 16.31] It is on this authority that he disregards sabbath restrictions imposed by the priesthood against both healing and eating, ignores their rituals of fasting and cleanliness and forgives sins in the interest of exercising human compassion. In a word, rejecting the authority of the Pharisees and scribes, Jesus appeals to authority that predates the establishment of the Judean monarchy, harking back to the earliest Hebraic codes and indeed before them to the customs of the habiru. In so doing, Jesus accounts himself a prophet in the line of the prophets, those who perpetuated the call to rachmones and dissent, and he is frequently addressed as such. "*As it is written in the prophets,*" [*Mark.* 1.2] Mark announces in beginning his account of Jesus' mission.

In basing his authority upon Moses and the prophets as opposed to that of the priesthood, Jesus is decisive. "*Think not that I am come to destroy the law or the prophets,*" Jesus himself assures his listeners in a passage that has confounded more than one commentator, "*I am not come to destroy, but to fulfill.*" [*Matthew.* 5.17] The assertion is fully comprehensible only in the sense that in overthrowing the restrictive laws of the priesthood, Jesus was preserving and fulfilling the ancient laws of his Jewish heritage. Railing against the injustices meted out by lawyers, scribes, Pharisees and the rich, Jesus employs much the same language as the prophets who preceded him. Overturning the tables of the money-changers in the temple, he is reinstating the ancient rule of one man, one half-shekel when making religious offerings. Drachmas, shekels and dinarii flying in every direction, here was Moses, in a later guise and setting, slaying the Egyptian soldier. In all these actions, the heritage of hebraic dissent is plainly visible. However nullified by priesthood and rulers during the period of the monarchy, Hebrew ideals of the call to justice continued to be deeply held in Jewish hearts, and were doubtless reflected in much of the daily life of ordinary people. It is to these people, "the poor of the land," that Jesus addressed himself. They above all had reason to preserve the ancient codes in which habiru/Hebraic society had been conceived.

So too, with rachmones. "*Verily I say unto you, Inasmuch as ye have done it unto one of the least of these my brethren, ye have done it unto me,*" [*Matthew.* 25.40] Jesus gives as a saying of the Son of man, thereby offering a succinct commentary on the operation of rachmones. "*Thou shalt love thy neighbor as thyself,* [*Matthew.* 19.19], he enjoins his followers, recalling a precept that lay at the heart of habiru/Hebrew culture. Feeling hurt at the injury of others and feeling love for one's fellows are certainly fundamental to rachmones.

For Jesus, however, love serves as a point of departure. Over and again Jesus emphasizes the spiritual holiness of love. The exercise of love becomes his mission. In loving one's enemies, turning the other cheek and rendering unto Caesar, Jesus makes love the essence of the "new wine" of belief that he is preaching. Thus renouncing the validity of dissent such as he himself had so unflinchingly demonstrated, Jesus distances himself from the Jewish prophets. Breaking away then both from the restrictive rituals of the priesthood and the rebellious fury of the prophets, he offers the poor in spirit a "new bottle" of religious devotion, designed to contain a wine from which all but love has been filtered away.

The consequences for Christianity were virtually inevitable. Despite early resistance and repeated sectarian and cultic rebellion, by and large, those who've followed in the footsteps of Jesus have attached themselves to the workings of corporate culture and to its authority. Caesar takes all. No longer safeguarded by dissent, loving thy neighbor increasingly assumes a missionary posture, therewith diluting the empathetic spontaneity of rachmones. One can readily appreciate the enormous value of Jesus' mission in the evolution of human awareness. It must have been apparent to the carpenter from Nazareth that the world at large was ready neither for rachmones nor for dissent. Love offered a middle path. It had to be, and he gave his life to make it so. A doctrine of love notwithstanding, in rendering one's physical life unto Caesar, it is easy to understand a festering sense of anger and frustration being directed against those heirs of the habiru who steadfastly have declined to go along with the arrangement.

[110] The innovative benefits of Hebraic dissent are not of course confined exclusively to the works of seminal thinkers such as Einstein, Freud and Marx. In his meteoric rise to stardom, Elvis Presley owed more than a little to the songwriting team of Mike Stoller and Jerry Leiber, two socially and politically irreverent Jews from Baltimore. Stoller's and Leiber's songs fueled the rock revolution in American and world music. A couple of decades earlier, Superman had burst into the comic book scene from the pens of Jerry Siegel and Joe Shuster, a pair of Jews from Cleveland. First and foremost of the super-heroes, the Kryptonian refugee made his debut in an outright subversion of corporate order. *"The first Superman appearance ended abruptly with the hero embarked on an even more radical campaign* [than previously in the same issue]: *fighting corruption in the United States government. In a continued story that may remind readers of recent events in the real world, Superman discovers that a lobbyist and a corrupt senator are engaged in a deal to sell arms to one side in a Latin American war. The munitions manufacturer behind the plot reforms after Superman forces him to fight in the front lines."* Les Daniels, in his survey, *DC Comics: A Celebration of the World's Favorite Comic Book Heroes,* 1995. Archetypal pop singer and archetypal super-hero, together they leavened the emergence of a major cultural transition, a gift of rachmones, wrapped in dissent, albeit liberally spiced with highly marketable schmaltz.

Through an uninterrupted lineage of satire and laughter, comedians have added their own talents to freeing cultural values in 20th century America. Since, almost by definition, comedy functions as a form of dissent, it is no surprise to find Jewish comedians playing a significant role in this medium as well. Charlie Chaplin, the Marx Brothers, Ritz Brothers, 3 Stooges, Eddie Cantor, Jack Benny, George Jessel, Milton Berle, Jerry Lewis, Mel Brooks, Carl Reiner, George Burns, Woody Allen, Danny Kaye, Mort Sahl, Sid Caesar, Zero Mostel, Jackie Gleason, Bette Midler, Billy Crystal, Jerry Seinfeld, Mike Nichols, Elaine May, among many others, all attest to the impact that Jewish dissent has had upon American, and thereby too, world culture. None with greater effect than Lenny Bruce, and Lenny was quite clear in what he was about.

"My humor is mostly indictment," Bruce asserted. "I'm a surgeon with a scalpel for false values," practicing a "comedy of dissent." Following in the footsteps of Allen Ginsberg, the Jewish poet who "broke the barrier between culture and dissent,." Lenny went much farther. Earning him a place, Ronald K.L. Collins & David M. Skover observe in *The Trials of Lenny Bruce: The Fall and Rise of an American Icon,* 2002, as "the celebrated high priest of comic dissent." A newspaper ad for a film of Bruce's life, on the other hand, hailed Lenny as a "major prophet." And so he was. In an unrelenting assault upon hypocrisy and repression, Lenny clearly belonged less in the line of the priests than the prophets. In venues that span the stretch between academic halls and city streets, their voice has never been stilled.

[111] Reprinted in *The Nation,* August 4, 2003. Arthur Miller's remarkable autobiography, *Time Bends: A Life,* 1987, is an extraordinary tribute to the vitality of the creative lyric when inspired by a spirit of dissent.

[112] When awarded the Nobel Prize for literature in 1978, Isaac Bashevis Singer attributed the creativity of Yiddish to its origins in the Jewish diaspora and a view of the world that was enhanced by statelessness. Yiddish, said Singer in his acceptance speech, is "*a language of exile, without a land, without frontiers, not supported by any government, a language which possesses no words for weapons, ammunition, military exercises, war tactics. There is a quiet humor in Yiddish,*" Singer went on to observe, "*and a gratitude for every day of life, every crumb of success, each encounter of love. In a figurative way, Yiddish is the wise and humble language of us all, the idiom of a frightened and hopeful humanity.*" In a word, the language of rachmones. Quoted in Richard Lederer, *A Man of My Words: Reflections on the English Language.* 2003.

[113] Here too, in passing beyond the confines of religion, relative at least to Catholics and Protestants, the Jews are a step ahead of the game. Most potentially terrifying of all to the true Christian believer is an unconscious suspicion that Judaism might in effect amount to atheism. It is not only Christ who is denied in

this scenario, but God himself. The suspicion is well-founded. In 1991, James Patterson and Peter Kim surveyed a representative sample of Americans, inquiring about their tastes and values. When they asked people if they believed in God, 97% of Protestants said yes, as did 96% of Catholics, but only 87% of Jews. Upon further questioning, the differences turned out to be much greater. Whereas 73% of Protestants and 65% of Catholics were "very sure of God's existence," only 27% of Jews agreed. Other responses elicited by Patterson and Kim follow the same pattern. 91% of both Catholics and Protestants believed that "God created the universe." Among Jews only 56% held this belief. Whereas only 7% of Protestants and 6% of Catholics described themselves as being "not at all religious," 30% of Jews did so. When asked if they "went to church/synagogue often when growing up," 67% of Protestants responded positively and 78% of Catholics, but only 31% of Jews. Most significantly, when the pollsters asked people if, "Less than 20% of [their] life [was] influenced by religious beliefs," while only 13% of Protestants and 15% of Catholics felt this to be the case, a full 51% of Jews thought so. In the heritage of the habiru, the possibility of a life without God lingers not far beneath the surface of consciousness. Moses and all the prophets had their hands full persuading the habiru otherwise. Patterson and Kim published their findings in *The Day America Told the Truth,* 1991

The debate over the need for religion, or its desirability, can no longer be joined without reference to the work of Andrew Newberg. A neurologist at the University of Pennsylvania, Newberg conducted brainscans of Buddhist and Franciscan nuns during prayer and meditation, injecting a tracer that discloses brain activity at the moment of transcendence. In those moments, Newberg found, a portion of the parietal lobe is deactivated. This area of the brain constantly calculates the person's spatial orientation, providing a sense of where one's body is in the world, in relation to other beings and things. Turning off this area of the parietal lobe, Newberg observes, "creates a blurring of the self-other relationship. If they go far enough, they have a complete dissolving of the self, a sense of union, a sense of infinite spacelessness." In a word, bliss. The devout person or successful meditator no longer knows where he or she is in space and time. In this state the person feels at one with the universe, adrift in bliss, joined to god or to the ineffable. When religion is most deeply felt, it appears, the part of the brain that is vital to us in experiencing our life in the world is the part that we turn off. Alternatively, one may enhance one's sense of being in the world, awakening one's senses and the flow of energy in one's body beyond their ordinary state. Those who do so report experiences of ecstasy. Bliss, then, or ecstasy, one takes one's choice. See Andrew Newberg, Eugene D'Aquili and Vince Rause, *Why God Won't Go Away: Brain Science and the Biology of Belief.* 2002.

Around 200 a.d. a woman named Maria invents the kerotakis, the earliest known alchemical still. Maria also constructs and describes various other "ovens and apparatuses for cooking and distilling made of metal, clay and glass." Abandoning religious belief in the interests of cultivating the magical arts of physical transformation, and known as "the Prophetess," Maria was Jewish. See Raphael Patai. *The Jewish Alchemists: A History and Source Book.* 1994.

[114] Augustine. "On the Morals of the Catholic Church". 388 a.d.

Appendix A

In tracing a culture of equal justice along with care for the indigent, slave and stranger to pre-hebraic times among the habiru, I've relied principally on the impact of historical consistency. In 2008 however a shard of red clay pottery the size of a human hand was recovered from a city gate in a fortified city in Judah, Khirbet Qeiyafa, that offers concrete substantiation for an early ethic of rachmones.

Situated on a hill above the Valley of Elah, site of the historico-mythic contest between David and Goliath, the city has been identified with biblical Sha'arayim. Its short lived occupancy, along with the pottery shard itself dates in fact to the early 10th century b.c., conjectural timing as well of David's kingship in Judah.

While the script has been identified as Early Alphabetic/Proto-Phoenician/Proto-Canaanite, the text is clearly a form of Hebrew

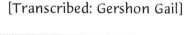
[Transcribed: Gershon Gail]

earlier than any other known. In a University of Haifa press release of 7 Jan. 2010, Gershon Gail proposes the following partially reconstructed translation:

you shall not do [it], but worship the [Lord].
Judge the sla[ve] and the wi[dow] / Judge the orph[an]
[and] the stranger. [Pl]ead for the infant / plead for the po[or and]
the widow.
Rehabilitate [the poor] at the hands of the king.
Protect the po[or and] the slave / [supp]ort the stranger.

Evidently addressed to the king, the measures of welfare and equal justice enjoined in this text will be repeated in the successive calls of biblical prophets down through the centuries of the Judean kingdom, then delivered by an heir to those prophets in a Sermon on the Mount.

Spanning millennia and crossing seas its message of impassioned empathy would be inscribed in our own times upon a bronze plaque affixed to the pedestal of the Statue of Liberty. The author, Emma Lazarus, was a Jewish-American with socialist leanings. However fitfully practiced, the call is preserved still in the heart of the Jewish ethos.

Appendix B

Short of attributing Moses' vision at the burning bush to a deliberate invention - too far out of keeping with priestly concerns; as a delusion - too reality oriented; or to the effects of longtime exposure to sunlight in semi-arid heat - a possibility, one can justifiably assume the workings of a hallucinogen at issue. Exploring the books of the Pentateuch, one need search no farther than *Exodus* for an explicit mention of a psychotropic plant, and when it occurs it is specifically attached to the name of Moses.

Exodus 30:22-31. Moreover the Lord spake unto Moses, saying, "Take thou also unto thee principal spices, of pure myrhh 500 shekels, and of sweet cinnamon half so much, even 250 shekels, and of sweet [smelling] kaneh bosem 250 shekels, and of cassia 500 shekels, after the shekel of the sanctuary, and of oil olive an hin: and thou shalt make it an oil of holy ointment, an ointment compounded after the art of the apothecary; it shall be an holy anointing oil. . . . throughout your generations.

250 shekels is estimated to have amounted to 9 pounds, contributing handsomely to a generous yield of holy anointing oil. In a flush perhaps of intentional delicacy the St. James version offers calamus as a translation for *kaneh bosem,* an identification that becomes accepted as a standard. With little linguistic affinity to calamus - a sour wetlands plant found elsewhere than in the Near East, *kaneh bosem* is readily translatable as cannabis, and the occurrence of cannabis has a long, honorable and very early history from Europe through the Middle East and on into Central Asia and Siberia.

The evidence for the use of hemp appearing as early as 10,000 b.c., in 3,000 b.c. we find a smoking cup in neolithic Romania with remnants of charred hemp seeds. 500 years later the temples of Margiana in Turkmenistan are provided with vessels dug into brick platforms containing the remains of poppy, cannabis and ephedra, harvested from the thickets of plants growing nearby. Around 1,800 b.c. that same potent cocktail fuels the forays of Vedic warriors into India who know it as the sacred soma/haoma. At about the same time Mesopotamian texts carry notices of *qunnabu/qunapy/qunubu /qunbu*. Later, c. 650 b.c. a recipe containing *qunnapu* for incense turns up in the library of the Assyrian king Ashurbanipal at Nineveh. In aramaic, lingua franca of the biblical Near East, the word for hemp was *kannabos*.

Its use known to have been favored by ancient shamans, and accorded sacred status among the hebrews, there's every reason then to suppose that the heady incense wafted aloft in the fumes of hotly heated holy oil likely inspired Moses in his vision of a supreme god who wished nothing other than to be known in existential splendor as "I am that I am."

[References and sources: Wikipedia article, *"Religious and spiritual use of cannabis."* See also: Chris Bennett, *"The Sacred Plant,"* Cannabis Health Journal, Sept., 2004.]

Epilogue

Aside from amplifying the preface, I've changed nothing in the original text of *Rachmones*. In the years since 2003, however, much has changed in my awareness of what Israel is all about. As, sadly and perhaps inexorably, Israel itself has changed.

"My awareness of the essential nature of Judaism," Albert Einstein stated late in 1938, "resists the idea of a Jewish state with borders, an army, and a measure of temporal power." And so, concluded Einstein, heir to hebraic origins in stateless citizenry, "The State idea is not in my heart." Nevertheless, when ten years later an Israeli state was declared, Einstein gave it his support. (In Walter Isaacson. *Einstein: His Life and Universe*, 2007.)

His misgivings notwithstanding, overcoming the "creative skepticism" for which Sigmund Freud lauded him, Einstein may well have hoped that the heritage of hebraic rachmones would outweigh the inevitable consequences of statehood. "The bond that has united the Jews for thousands of years and that unites them today," Einstein had observed in an interview with *Colliers* 11/26/38, "is, above all, the democratic ideal of social justice coupled with the ideal of mutual aid and tolerance among all men." In a word, rachmones. Knowing how profoundly ingrained it was in Jewish hearts and minds, Einstein could imagine rachmones operative even within statehood.

Concluding *Rachmones* in 2003, well aware of the inherent contradiction between humanity and statehood that has plagued our species for the past 5000 years, I succumbed to the same naively inspired hopefulness that Einstein had voiced so many decades earlier. Knowing the intensity of struggle for equal justice that began five millenniums ago in popular defections from bronze-age corporate society, a perspective to this day persisting in Jewish culture, I regarded Israel as a foothold for democracy in lands that little prized it. Israelis, I supposed, would not tolerate the demands for conformity and mindless patriotism that states make as a matter of course upon their citizens. I assumed that Israelis would retain the awareness of "stateless citizens" within the confines of their state.

A man whose "brilliance sprang from being a rebel and nonconformist who recoiled at any attempt to restrain his free expression," Einstein was wrong. And I was wrong. Fueled by a Jewish fundamentalism that's proving itself every bit as arrogant and ruthless as Christian and Muslim fundamentalism, Israel has slipped into the dehumanization from which no corporate enterprise, public or private, however well-intentioned, has ever succeeded fully in exempting itself.

It had to be. That a people who preserved the highest ideals of empathetic society should have fallen prey to the imperatives of "benefits and obedience" emphasizes the implacability of the corporate dynamic. Even accepting the inevitability of the outcome, I am sorry, so very sorry. In return, with no hope any longer for their state, my heart is warmed by coffee shop voices in Tel Aviv, after 200 generations of rachmones and dissent still echoing the admonitions of the prophets.

The passions of rachmones, ubuntu, aloha along with the many other ethnic expressions of human empathy increasingly resonate in the consciousness of people everywhere. Meanwhile the greening of hearts prompted by global concerns in preserving the planetary habitat effectively transcends all boundaries to embrace everyone in a grand awakening of empathy. Stateless citizens all, along with "citizen of the world" Albert Einstein, owning the earth itself as their home.

Relying upon the manifold evidences of collaborative engagement that he observes in so many contexts, primatologist Frans de Waal envisions an Age of Empathy in our hominid future. Whatever catastrophes may be awaiting us on our way there, eventually it must come to pass, necessarily as a matter of survival, blessedly in a bounty of well-being.

Kapa'au, HI 2/19/10